# MARKSTRAT
# A Marketing
# Strategy Game

$9.00 $8.01

JEAN-CLAUDE LARRÉCHÉ, *Associate Professor of Marketing, INSEAD*

HUBERT GATIGNON, *Faculty Assistant, CEDEP*

*The Scientific Press,* THE STANFORD BARN, PALO ALTO, CA 94304

# Participant's Manual

MARKSTRAT
Jean-Claude Larréché
Hubert Gatignon

Copyright © 1977 by CEDEP / INSEAD
(*Centre Européen d'Education Permanente / The European Institute of Business Administration*)

Published by The Scientific Press

Library of Congress Catalogue Card Number  LC77-89287

ISBN 0-89426-010-3

Cover design and illustrations by Rogondino Associates
Typography by The Scientific Press
Printed in the USA

# Preface

MARKSTRAT is a simulation game specifically designed for teaching marketing strategy concepts. Compared to the more traditional marketing management games, its main distinctive features are:

1. a longer term perspective

2. an emphasis on segmentation, positioning and repositioning issues

3. the opportunity to manage and expand the product line through the modification of existing brands or the introduction of new ones

4. the availability of a comprehensive set of fifteen marketing research studies

5. the graphical representation of brand similarities and preferences through perceptual mapping

6. a more dynamic environment, reflected by different product/market life cycles, the creation of a new market, inflation, price controls, and changes in the levels of productivity.

For maximum effectiveness, participation in MARKSTRAT requires familiarity with basic marketing concepts previously acquired through formal courses or practical experience. The simulation is best suited for the end of a basic marketing management course, or more advanced marketing strategy courses. MARKSTRAT has now been extensively used with constant success in several graduate and executive programs.

MARKSTRAT has been tested and updated over a period of two years at the Centre Européen d'Education Permanente (CEDEP) and at the European Institute of Business Administration (INSEAD) in Fontainebleau. Its development was made possible by the financial support of these institutions. We would particularly like to thank Uwe Kitzinger, Dean of INSEAD, and Salvatore Teresi, Director General of CEDEP, for their encouragement in the development and publication of MARKSTRAT.

We would also like to thank Alain Charpentreau and Paule Villain for their participation in the programming, and Thierry Gauthier for his help in designing the visual aids. The current version of MARKSTRAT has benefited from the comments of Dean Harper W. Boyd, Jr. at Tulane University, Reza Moinpour at the University of Washington, David B. Montgomery at Stanford University, Deigan Morris and David Weinstein at INSEAD. Our special appreciation goes to Edward C. Strong, Tulane University, who has extensively tested, used and contributed to various versions of the MARKSTRAT manual and programs. To all of them we would like to express our gratitude.

J.-C. Larréché/H. Gatignon
INSEAD/CEDEP
Fontainebleau France
June 1977

# To The Instructor

The MARKSTRAT programs were originally written in BASIC for the Hewlett-Packard 2000 Access computer. They have already been adapted to some other computer systems, and can be used with minor modifications on practically any computer configuration offering a BASIC compiler.

A Teacher's manual is available from the publisher. It contains, in particular, a description of the pedagogical process of MARKSTRAT, a set of transparencies for classroom presentation, instructions on running the simulation, and a detailed description of the MARKSTRAT model. A computer magnetic tape containing the MARKSTRAT programs is also available from the publisher.

In addition, a French version of MARKSTRAT is also available. Interested instructors should write directly to the authors for more details.

# Contents

**1. Why a Simulation**     1
Pedagogical Games     1
The MARKSTRAT Simulation     2

**2. The MARKSTRAT World**     5
The Industry     5
The Organization of the Firm     5
    (The Marketing Department as a Profit Center)*
The Market Structure and its Environment     7
Products     7
    (Physical Characteristics of Brands Commercialized at the Beginning of the Simulation)
Consumers     9
Distribution, Pricing, Sales Force     10
Advertising, Marketing Research, Research & Development     11
    (Feasible Ranges of the Physical Characteristics, Values for Sonites & Vodites)
Productivity Gains     12
    (Productivity Gains)
Economic Environment     13

**3. Designing and Implementing a Marketing Strategy**     15
Marketing Research     15
    (Initial Cost of Marketing Research Studies)
Positioning, Repositioning, and Segmentation     18
    (Perceptual Mapping of Brand Similarities & Preferences)
Implementation of the Marketing Strategy     22
    (The Marketing-R & D Interface)

**4. Operating Instructions**     25
The Company Report     27
The Decision Form     29
    (Sample Decision Form)
    (Specifications of Perceptual Objectives from Semantic Scale Data)
The Budgeting Form     35
    (Sample Budgeting Form)
The Planning Form     39
    (Sample Planning Form)

**5. Final Considerations**     43
    (Convention for Brand and R & D Project Names)
    (General Background Information)

**Appendix A.  Sample Company Report**     49
**Appendix B.  Sample Marketing Research Studies**     55
**Appendix C.  Blank Forms**     61

*(Exhibits)*

# 1
# Why A Simulation?

In general, the purpose of a simulation is to test alternative actions without incurring the cost or the risk of implementing them in a real setting. The use of simulation requires a model that is a simplified representation of reality. Although models can be expressed in several forms (such as physical, graphical, or verbal), they are most frequently represented by mathematical relations. The structure of the model, the mathematical equations used and the values of its parameters, are defined from data relevant to the situation being modeled.

The huge number of variables interacting in a social or business situation cannot all be included in a model—even when they can be defined—because it would be impractical and technically difficult to attempt to do so. The art of modeling, therefore, lies in the selection of only the most important variables in a given process and in the definition of their relationships. The resulting model can, then, be programmed and run on a computer to economically test alternative actions and to answer "what if" types of questions.

There has been extensive development of simulation models in marketing.[1] They are, by definition, incomplete representations of reality and cannot incorporate unexpected competitive actions or drastic changes in the environment. They are, however, empirically based, and good models have a high enough predictive validity so that a satisfactory plan, tested on a simulation model, may be implemented with success in the real situation.

## Pedagogical Games

Pedagogical games are a particular type of simulation for which the main objective is to learn and to practice concepts, techniques, and decision-making processes. They have been developed for such diverse areas of application as political science, economics, history, psychology, sociology, and business.[2] The simulation model used in a business game

---

[1] See, for instance: P. Kotler and R. L. Schultz, "Marketing Simulations: Review and Prospects," Journal of Business, Vol. 43, No. 3 (July 1970), pp. 237–295; D. B. Montgomery and G. L. Urban, Management Science in Marketing, Englewood Cliffs, N.J.: Prentice-Hall, 1969; P. Kotler, Marketing Decision Making: A Model Building Approach, New York: Holt, Rinehart and Winston, 1971.

[2] See, for instance, D. W. Zuckerman and R. E. Horn, The Guide to Simulation Games for Education and Training, Cambridge, Mass.: Information Resources Inc., 1970.

represents a business situation in such a way that the *learning* of concepts, techniques, and decision-making processes can be transposed into real business situations. Games, however, as opposed to the simulation models used in companies, are not based on specific empirical data. They usually simulate a fictitious industry and use synthetic data, so that the *numerical results* obtained in the process of playing the game cannot be transposed into real life situations.

In a typical business game several companies are in competition in a given industry, and each company is managed by a group of students. Each group makes decisions about various aspects of their company's management for a given period of "simulated time," which may run from one month to one year. When all groups have independently made their decisions, they are entered in a computer-based simulation model. The results for each company are returned to the corresponding group. Often information may be purchased, including information on competing companies. The game is, thus, played over several simulated periods in which each team tries to maximize its objectives (for instance, sales, market share, and profits.) The objectives are, of course, achieved much more systematically and successfully by considering and applying concepts previously developed in lectures.

In participating in a pedagogical game, one is immediately immersed in a dynamic, competitive situation. Many months of activity are simulated in a short time, and rapid feedback is obtained on all decisions. Learning in the new situations take place through trial and error and through the acquisition of additional information. The behavior of competitors also affects results and must, accordingly, be taken into account. Finally, one must cooperate with the other members of his "management" team.

A simulation in the form of a business game is a pedagogical device wherein learning takes place in a stimulating competitive environment. Compared to the more traditional case study approach, it provides a more dynamic situation within which actions are to be tested and modified. Compared to practice in a real business situation, a game satisfactorily reproduces its main aspects, while providing faster feedback at lower cost and lower risk.

### The MARKSTRAT Simulation

MARKSTRAT is a simulation game and, as such, has the following characteristics:

1. It is a simplification of reality. The computerized model used in MARKSTRAT contains a set of relationships that simulate real business phenomena. However, in order to maximize its pedagogical effectiveness, it includes only the main elements of those phenomena.

2. It represents a specific business environment: the MARKSTRAT world. This environment possesses its own characteristics of products, market sizes, distribution channels, etc. Accordingly, decisions should be based solely on information gathered in MARK-

STRAT, and not on data obtained from existing markets or products—which would not be compatible with the situations modeled in the game.

3. It provides a realistic learning setting. In MARKSTRAT, it is possible to test various propositions gathered through prior business education or practice. The experience gained during the course of the simulation can then be transferred to real business situations.

MARKSTRAT is, however, different in several respects from other business games that you may know. It has been designed, primarily, to apply and test marketing *strategy* concepts. It focuses on the various marketing functions of the firm and on the elements of the environment that have the greatest impact on these functions. Particular emphasis is placed on the main elements of marketing strategy: segmentation, and positioning. Product, distribution, pricing, advertising and sales force policy are considered as the means of implementing an overall marketing strategy that is formulated at the corporate level. This strategy emphasis is supported by the length of the simulated periods, which are of one year's duration. The simulation is usually run over six to ten periods, which gives us the longer time horizons necessary for adequately testing marketing strategies. Other functions of the firm (such as finance, production, and R&D) intervene only as support for or constraints upon the firm's marketing strategy.

The MARKSTRAT game also incorporates a large number of marketing research studies, which may be purchased by the competing companies to assist in decision-making. In addition to more classical studies (such as consumer surveys, consumer panels, distribution panels, and market forecasts), MARKSTRAT makes available more sophisticated information (such as perceptual maps, sales force experiments, and advertising experiments).

The general setting of MARKSTRAT is presented in chapter two, "The MARKSTRAT World." Chapter three shows how a marketing strategy can be designed and implemented within the MARKSTRAT game. Chapter four will describe in detail how to operate one of the companies of MARKSTRAT, how to report decisions, and how to interpret yearly results. Finally, the last chapter gives some recommendations concerning participation in the MARKSTRAT simulation.

# 2
# The Markstrat World

The MARKSTRAT simulation does not claim to accurately represent a particular industry or market. It relates to an artificial community of approximately 250 million inhabitants whose monetary unit is the MMU (MARKSTRAT Monetary Unit, symbolized by $). This MARKSTRAT world behaves globally like most markets, and all general marketing principles accumulated either through experience or from marketing textbooks are relevant. However, MARKSTRAT, like any specific country, market, or industry, also has its own pecularities. It is, thus, important both to read carefully the description of the MARKSTRAT world that follows and to interpret the information you will receive in the course of the game concerning the pecularities of the products you are about to manage and the environment in which you are to operate.

## The Industry

The MARKSTRAT World consists of five competing companies that manufacture and market a consumer durable good comparable to an electronic entertainement product. Each firm is managed by a team. At the beginning of the game, each firm markets two brands but can modify or withdraw existing brands and introduce new ones as the game evolves. In any year, it may commercialize up to five brands altogether. Each firm starts from a different initial situation, which corresponds to the overall structure of the industry. This is reflected by such things as differences in the market shares, consumer awareness levels, and distribution coverage of the various companies' brands. The marketing strategy of each firm should be adapted to its peculiar situation within the industry. For the same reason, the performance of the different companies over the successive periods of the simulation cannot be compared in absolute terms; but, more appropriately, with respect to their initial situation.

## Organization of the Firm

In each of the five firms, the marketing department is considered to be a profit center responsible for the design and implementation of marketing strategy as well as for marketing operations. In this privileged situation, the marketing department is responsible for the overall orientation of the company to its markets, and it must interact with other departments of the firm. In each period, it must request a certain level of production for each of its brands from the production department. The quantities requested and produced are charged to the marketing department at an internal transfer price corresponding to the production cost. The marketing department is also responsible for inventory holding costs incurred from overproduction. In a similar fashion, the marketing department may ask the R & D department to work on specific projects, in which case it bears the expenditures involved within its budget.

The performance of the marketing department as a profit center is appraised on the *net marketing contribution* represented in Exhibit 1. This

EXHIBIT 1
The Marketing Department as a Profit Center

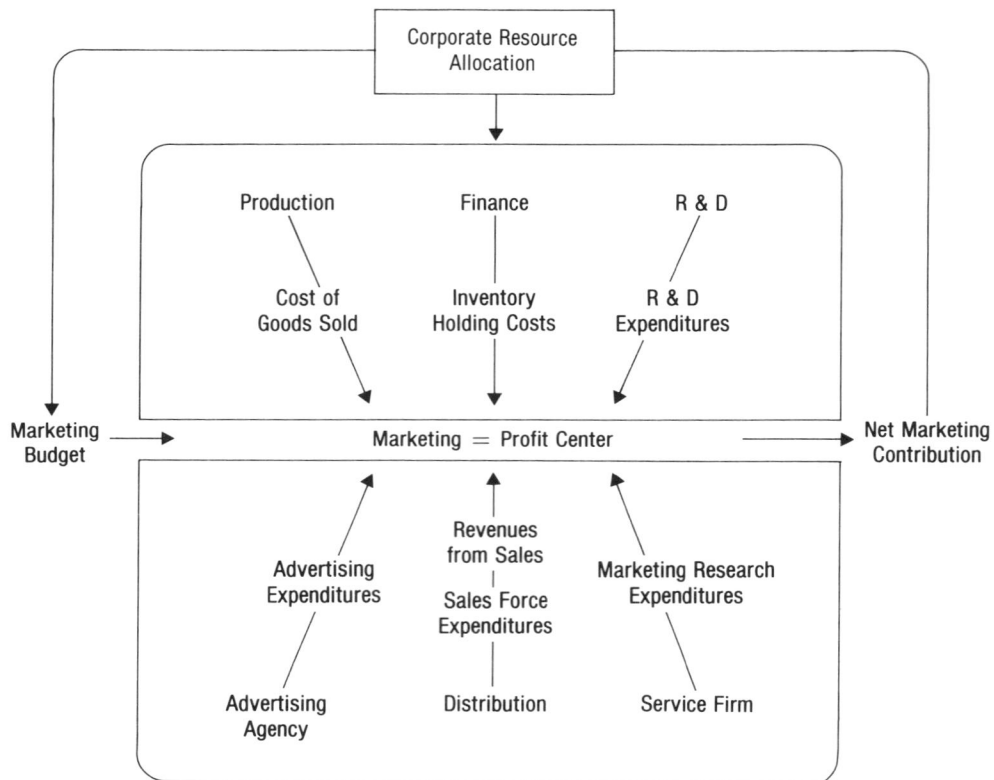

net marketing contribution is defined as total revenues from sales, minus: cost of goods sold (based on transfer prices), inventory holding costs, and R & D, advertising, sales force, and marketing research expenditures. The marketing department is given a budget for the following period to cover R & D, advertising, sales force, and marketing research expenditures. This budget is partly based upon net marketing contribution in the preceding period, but firms may also negotiate changes with the game administrator, on the basis of a well-defined marketing plan.

The marketing departments in MARKSTRAT have a considerable influence upon the general strategy of their firms. They can give directives to other departments, such as production and R & D, but are responsible for the inefficiencies that may result. They are not concerned with other activities of the firm (such as credit management, capital investments, financial reporting, purchasing, or plant management). These services are performed by other profit centers. For instance, increases in production capacity are made by the production and finance departments, according to the requirements of the marketing department. The net marketing contribution is used at the corporate level to cover these activities, as well as fixed costs, financial charges, and profits. As far as the marketing department is concerned, the net marketing contribution only represents a measure of performance, while its yearly budget represents available funds than can be used freely to attain self-assigned objectives.

## Market Structure and Its Environment

The MARKSTRAT market has grown slowly over the last twenty years. After several significant technological breakthroughs, the products have increasingly appealed to a wider audience, and the market has recently achieved an even greater rate of growth. It is now a well structured market with five principal competitors and established channels of distribution. Over the years, the firms have acquired an understanding of consumer behavior, industry practices, and characteristics of the environment similar to the information presented in this manual.

**Products.** The generic product in the MARKSTRAT market is called the "Sonite," a consumer durable good comparable to an electronic entertainment product. It is relatively sophisticated technically but, in contrast with what has occurred in the last twenty years, no major basic technological changes are expected in the future. Sonite brands are differentiated mainly in terms of six physical characteristics, and only these principal characteristics will be considered in the course of the game. They are:

1. Weight (*kg*)
2. Design (*index*)
3. Volume (*dm³*)
4. Maximum frequency (1000 *hz*)
5. Power (*W*)
6. Cost ($)

All these characteristics can be accurately measured for a given Sonite, either by standard measurement instruments or by well-defined procedures. The cost characteristic of a given Sonite represents the average unit cost on its first production run, assuming a production batch of 100,000 units.

Each firm currently distributes two brands. The ten Sonite brands, which are available at the start of the simulation, and their characteristics are listed

EXHIBIT 2
Physical Characteristics of Brands
Commercialized at the Start of the Simulation

| Brand Name | Physical Characteristics | | | | | |
| | Weight | Design | Volume | Maximum Frequency | Power | Cost |
| | (kg) | (index) | (dm³) | (1000 Hz) | (W) | ($) |
|---|---|---|---|---|---|---|
| SAMA | 10 | 8 | 30 | 25 | 10 | 100 |
| SALT | 12 | 9 | 37 | 25 | 30 | 125 |
| SEMI | 17 | 7 | 50 | 30 | 80 | 160 |
| SELF | 15 | 5 | 60 | 40 | 90 | 200 |
| SIRO | 10 | 3 | 50 | 20 | 10 | 50 |
| SIBI | 11 | 8.5 | 35 | 25 | 20 | 100 |
| SOLD | 17 | 7 | 50 | 30 | 70 | 165 |
| SONO | 10 | 3 | 70 | 20 | 90 | 180 |
| SUSI | 10 | 3 | 50 | 25 | 20 | 70 |
| SULI | 15 | 6 | 40 | 20 | 70 | 175 |

in Exhibit 2. It is easy to recognize the origin of the brands from their names. Each brand name is made up of four letters, and the first letter is "S" for Sonite. The second letter of the brand name identifies the company in the following way, "A" for company 1, "E" for company 2, "I" for company 3, "O" for company 4, and "U" for company 5. The last two letters are selected by each firm to generate different brand names. It is, for instance, easy to recognize that brands "SIRO" and "SIBI" in Exhibit 2 belong to company 3.

It is generally thought that the MARKSTRAT firms will modify their brands or introduce new ones in the coming years, in order to better meet the needs of the market segments. These changes will represent variations on the six main characteristics described above. Brand improvements and new brand introductions naturally depend upon the willingness and ability of the firms to launch R & D projects. All new brand names should follow the conventions previously described, namely: first letter "S," second letter should identify the company, and the last two letters can be freely selected as long as all brands have different names. The selected name has no influence on the market response to the brand.

More recently, there has been talk in the industry about a completely new product, the "Vodite." The idea for the product comes from a basic technological breakthrough made in the space industry under governmental contracts. The MARKSTRAT industry is certainly the most likely to manufacture and distribute the Vodite because of its technological and marketing expertise.

Although the scientific bases are known and available, substantial R & D efforts are required for the development of a Vodite brand. From preliminary information available, its main physical characteristics would be:

1. Autonomy (*m*)
2. Maximum frequency (1000 *Hz*)
3. Diameter (*mm*)
4. Design (*index*)
5. Weight (*g*)
6. Cost ($).

The Vodites would satisfy an entirely different need than that of the Sonites, and there would be no interaction between the two types of products at the sales level, although they would be distributed through the same channels. If a Vodite brand is developed and launched, the reaction of the market to this new product, the rate of adoption, and the equilibrium level of sales would remain entirely unknown at the present time, although development of the Vodite market may be similar to the historical development of the Sonite markets. Vodite brand names follow the same convention as the Sonite brand names, except that the first letter should be a "V," for Vodite.

**Consumers.** The target markets in MARKSTRAT are households and individuals over 18 years of age. The opinion of experts, confirmed by several studies undertaken by the firms, is that one can distinguish five segments with different characteristics and significantly different purchasing behavior.

*Segment 1: The Buffs.* Persons who are enthusiastic and very knowledgeable about the products. They are primarily concerned with quality and technical features.

*Segment 2: The Singles.* Persons who live alone. Although they are less technically competent than the Buffs, they demand good performance from a product they may use more than the average consumer.

*Segment 3: The Professions.* Persons who have a higher level of education and high incomes. They tend to be more independent in their occupation and to engage in many social activities. Their purchase of the product is partially motivated by social status needs.

*Segment 4: The High Earners.* Persons who have high incomes but do not possess the higher level of education or occupational independence of the individuals in Segment 3.

*Segment 5: Others.* Persons who do not belong to the above groups. This segment represents the largest proportion of the population. However, in the past it has known a significantly lower penetration of Sonite products than other segments.

The order of these groups corresponds to the priority of attribution of an individual to a segment. For instance, the persons in the "High Earners" group are those who have high incomes but do not qualify as members of the three preceding segments: "The Buffs," "The Singles," or "The Professions." The resulting segmentation is thus mutually exclusive and exhaustive.

"The Buffs" currently constitute the largest segment in terms of Sonite unit sales, and represent 30% of the market. They are followed by Segment 3 (20%), Segment 5 (19%), Segment 4 (16%), and Segment 2 (15%). It is, however, common knowledge in the industry that the five segments are at different stages of their development. This is partly reflected by different growth rates. While the overall Sonite market has enjoyed an average annual growth rate of 35% over the last three years, Segment 1 has been stagnant, Segments 2 and 5 have grown at 25–30%, and Segments 3 and 4 have grown at twice that rate.

**Distribution.** All products may be directly distributed through three different channels:

*Channel 1: Specialty stores.* They make the bulk of their turnover from Sonite-type products and provide specialized services.

*Channel 2: Electric Appliances stores.* They carry Sonites only as an addition to their main electric appliances lines.

*Channel 3: Department stores.* They handle a wide variety of merchandise and may have a department carrying the Sonites.

It is estimated that there are 3,000 specialty stores, 35,000 electric appliances stores and 4,000 department stores in MARKSTRAT, all of which can potentially distribute the Sonite and Vodite brands. Each of the channels differs in terms of penetration of Sonite brands, and attraction of different types of clientele. Differences exist between the margins obtained by the stores in each of the three types of channels, and they are mainly due to differences in the service level and the quantities purchased. These margins, expressed as a percentage of the recommended retail price, are approximately constant across brands for a given channel type. Their values are 40%, 35%, and 40% respectively for channels 1, 2 and 3. These margins represent an equilibrium that has evolved over the years, and neither distributors nor Sonite manufacturers have any motivation to disrupt the equilibrium.

**Pricing.** The MARKSTRAT companies provide recommended retail prices for each of their brands. These prices are generally respected by all channels except for promotions. These promotions are of short duration and represent only a small proportion of sales. The average retail price in any one year is, thus, close to the recommended retail price. Over the last three years, prices of Sonites have increased regularly, and have followed inflation.

**Sales Force.** The sales force of a MARKSTRAT company is organized by channel type in order to better meet the specific needs of the channels. Each salesman carries the company's entire line of brands. A company may naturally change the size of its sales force at a cost representing training, firing, and salary expenses. Changes in the number of salesmen are expected to have an influence on the distribution coverage of the company's brands. In addition, each year a company may modify the allocation of its sales force to specific distribution channels at no significant cost.

**Advertising.** The practice in the MARKSTRAT industry is to advertise specific brands, rather than a generic company brand. Although the major purpose of advertising has been to promote specific brands, the advertising efforts of the MARKSTRAT companies have largely contributed to the development of the Sonite market.

Advertising expenditures for Sonite brands are of two types. The bulk of the advertising budget is devoted to the purchase of media space or time. The rest of the budget is spent on advertising research. On average, the MARKSTRAT companies spend ten percent of their sales on advertising. In general, five percent of their advertising budgets are allocated to advertising research performed by their advertising agencies and concerned mainly with creative work, media selection studies, and copy testing. They may try to change the allocation between media expenses and research expenses in an effort to improve advertising effectiveness.

**Marketing Research.** Fifteen studies can be purchased by the MARKSTRAT companies from outside marketing service firms. They are described in the next chapter.

**Research and Development.** The marketing department of a firm may request the R & D department to develop specific projects in order to improve existing brands or to introduce new ones. A request to the R & D department consists of a project name, a budget, and values of the physical characteristics that the researched product should possess.

The names of R & D projects are made up of five letters. The first letter is always "P," for Project, and the second letter identifies the type of product being developed: "S," for Sonites, and "V," for Vodites. The last three letters can be selected by the firms to identify specific projects. "PSETA" and "PVOTE" are, for instance, valid names for a Sonite and a Vodite, respectively. There is no need for the name of an R & D project to correspond with the name of an existing or planned brand, and all current and past R & D projects must have different names. In the past, each firm has successfully completed two R & D projects corresponding to the brands commercialized in Period 0. Their names are made of the letter P followed by the corresponding brand name.

The budget for a given project represents the investment that marketing is ready to make for the R & D department to try to develop that specified product in the coming year. It will, naturally, be subtracted from the marketing budget. In specifying the physical characteristics of the desired product, the marketing department should, obviously, evaluate the market opportunities for any alternative offerings. The values of the physical characteristics for R & D projects should be prescribed in the relevant units, and the feasible ranges for each dimension are indicated in Exhibit 3. The last characteristic, both for Sonites and Vodites, represents the average unit production cost in manufacturing the first 100,000 units of the new product.

Therefore, the R & D department has to develop a product with given physical characteristics, but it also has to find the raw materials and the technology that will allow production at the specified cost. Obviously, the more stringent this economic constraint, the more difficult it will be for the R & D department to develop the corresponding product. If the product is eventually

EXHIBIT 3
Feasible Ranges of the Physical Characteristics
Values for Sonites and Vodites

|  | Physical Characteristics | Feasible Range |
|---|---|---|
| Sonites: | Weight (Kg) | 10 – 20 |
|  | Design (index) | 3 – 10 |
|  | Volume (dm$^3$) | 20 – 100 |
|  | Maximum Frequency (1000 Hz) | 5 – 50 |
|  | Power (W) | 5 – 100 |
|  | Cost ($) | 100 – 600 |
| Vodites: | Autonomy (m) | 5 – 100 |
|  | Maximum Frequency (1000 Hz) | 5 – 20 |
|  | Diameter (mm) | 10 – 100 |
|  | Design (index) | 3 – 10 |
|  | Weight (g) | 10 – 100 |
|  | Cost ($) | 50 – 500 |

marketed, the transfer price will be determined on the basis of this cost. But, it may vary as a function of the quantities produced and the learning effects, as well as inflation.

Up to four projects may be simultaneously given to the R & D department. If a project is not successfully completed in one year and is unlikely to be in the future, because the product specifications are too stringent, this will be indicated in a message from the R & D department. If a project is not successfully completed for lack of funds, the R & D department will supply an estimate of the additional budget that it would need to bring the project to completion. If an R & D project is not successfully completed in one year, it may be pursued in the following periods. The likelihood of the success of a project depends primarily on the *cumulative* expenditures incurred and the degree of similarity between the desired products and the firm's existing ones. The R & D department is also a profit center and, thus, will use all funds provided to it in the course of the year.

Conceptually, R & D project expenses include not only the expense required to develop the prototype but also the research and evaluation necessary to find components and potential suppliers, make technical evaluations, provide production line planning, and produce prototypes. In period 0, a successful R & D project for a Sonite would generally cost between $100,000 and $1,000,000, depending upon the degree of difference between the desired characteristics of the project and the characteristics of existing products. In order to develop a Vodite, industry experts believe that it will be necessary to spend a minimum of $2,000,000 on R & D.

**Productivity Gains.** The manufacturing costs of the products tend to decrease as a result of productivity improvements gained through experience, although this effect may be offset by inflation. Greater changes in manufacturing costs may be obtained by undertaking appropriate R & D projects, for which it is necessary to change only the cost characteristics of

EXHIBIT 4
Productivity Gains

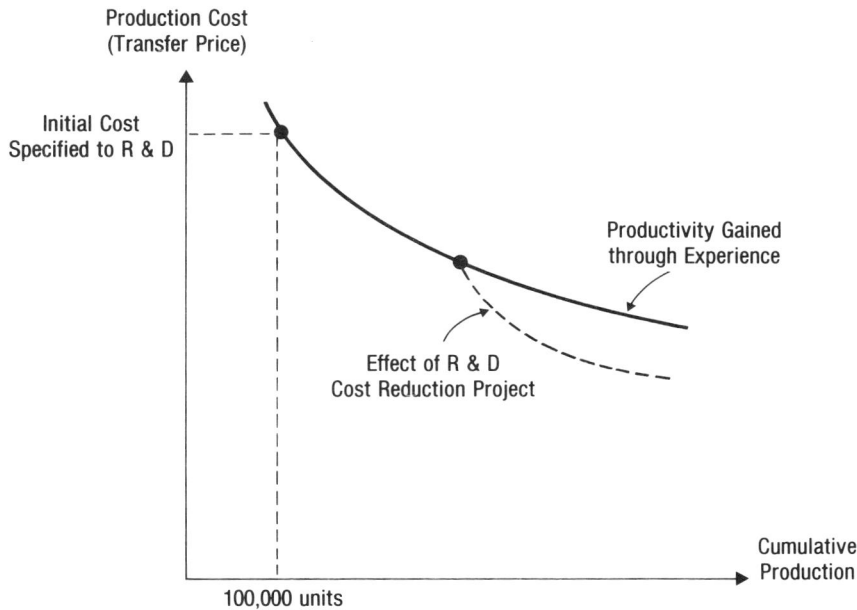

an otherwise unmodified product. Both of these effects are conceptually represented on Exhibit 4.

**Economic Environment.** The MARKSTRAT industry operates in an economy that is currently subject to an average inflation rate of nine percent. This inflation affects the manufacturing, advertising, sales force, R & D, and marketing research costs of the companies. In addition, price controls may be imposed on all brands by the government in order to try to reduce inflation.

# 3

# Designing & Implementing A Marketing Strategy

The MARKSTRAT game has been designed primarily to allow testing and implementation of marketing strategy concepts. Each simulated period lasts one year, which means that each decision a team makes covers an entire year, and the game is played over a minimum of six simulated years of operations. This implies, first, that long-term marketing strategies should be formulated so that their impact will be effectively tested. Second, it decreases the importance of many short-term marketing actions such as temporary promotions and media scheduling, which are therefore not considered in the game.

The design and implementation of a marketing strategy requires gathering information on the competitive market situation. This may be achieved in several ways. First, by carefully reading and assimilating the information contained in this manual. Second, by trying out various marketing actions in succession and learning through experience. Finally, by buying marketing research information from outside marketing service firms. Given some knowledge of market structure and behavior, a marketing strategy may be designed in terms of repositioning existing brands and positioning new brands with respect to the five consumer segments. Actions must then be taken at the level of the marketing-mix elements, R & D projects, and production planning in order to implement the marketing strategy selected. It should be clear from this three-stage process—gathering of information, design of a marketing strategy, and implementation of this strategy—that the management of the marketing mix should not be an end in itself but only a means of achieving a strategy. The main elements of these three stages will now be described in more detail.

## Marketing Research

The companies in the MARKSTRAT industry may buy up to 15 different marketing research studies in one annual period. The costs of these studies in the initial period are indicated in Exhibit 5, and they are expected to increase with inflation in the course of the game. The results from these

EXHIBIT 5
Initial Cost of Marketing Research Studies

| | | *Initial Cost* |
|---|---|---|
| *Study* 1: | Consumer Survey, Market S | $ 60,000 |
| *Study* 2: | Consumer Panel, Market S | 100,000 |
| *Study* 3: | Distribution Panel, Market S | 60,000 |
| *Study* 4: | Semantic Scales, Market S | 10,000 |
| *Study* 5: | Perceptual Mapping of Brands' Similarities and Preferences, Market S | 35,000 |
| *Study* 6: | Market Forecast, Market S | 20,000 |
| *Study* 7: | Consumer Survey, Market V | $ 40,000 |
| *Study* 8: | Consumer Panel, Market V | 70,000 |
| *Study* 9: | Distribution Panel, Market V | 50,000 |
| *Study* 10: | Semantic Scales, Market V | 10,000 |
| *Study* 11: | Market Forecast, Market V | 20,000 |
| *Study* 12: | Competitive Advertising Estimates | $ 30,000 |
| *Study* 13: | Competitive Sales Force Estimates | 15,000 |
| *Study* 14: | Sales Force Experiment | 24,000 |
| *Study* 15: | Advertising Experiment | 35,000 |

studies have different levels of errors attached to them, according to the methodology used and the sample size. An example of each of these studies is given in Appendix B.

**Study 1: Consumer Survey—Market S.** The "Market S" and "Market V" denominations refer to studies performed on Sonite and Vodite brands, respectively. Study 1 is a survey questionnaire administered to 3000 individuals. It gives brand awareness, purchase intentions, and shopping habit data for each of the five segments. The brand awareness figures represent the proportion of individuals who have unaided recall of a brand's name, and they are given for each Sonite brand currently on the market. The purchase intentions figures represent the proportion of individuals who would select a brand as their first choice if they were buying one within a year. These figures are also presented for each Sonite brand currently on the market. The shopping habit data give, for each channel type, the proportion of individuals who would choose this channel when shopping for a Sonite.

**Study 2: Consumer Panel—Market S.** This study provides the market shares, based on units sold, for each Sonite brand in each segment. The industry sales in each segment are also indicated, in thousand units.

**Study 3: Distribution Panel—Market S.** This study provides the market shares, based on units sold, for each Sonite brand in each channel. The industry sales in each distribution channel are also indicated, in thousand units.

**Study 4: Semantic Scales—Market S.** This study is based on a semantic differential questionnaire administered to a sample of 600 individuals.

Several semantic scales, such as the following one corresponding to the physical characteristics of Sonites, were presented to the respondents:

Lightest    1   2   3   4   5   6   7    Heaviest

Each respondent was asked to rate each brand according to the way he perceived the brand on that characteristic. He was also asked to indicate his most preferred (or "ideal") point on each scale, and to rank the scales in terms of their importance to him. The reported results are the median scale values for each brand and for the segment ideal points on the three scales which were ranked as most important.

**Study 5: Perceptual Mapping of Brand's Similarities and Preferences —Market S.** This study provides a joint-space configuration obtained by non-metric multidimensional scaling.[3] It relies on similarity and preference data on the complete set of Sonite brands obtained through interviews with a sample of 200 individuals. It first gives the minimum number of dimensions that were sufficient to provide a good fit to the data, as well as a likely interpretation of the axes based on semantic scale responses. The study then provides the graphical representation in this space of the perceptual positioning of the Sonite brands and the segments' ideal points. An example of such a perceptual map and further details on its interpretation will be given in the next section.

**Study 6: Market Forecast—Market S.** This study provides an estimate of the market size, in thousands of units of Sonites, for the next period and gives a breakdown by segment. It relies on market extrapolation and assumes stable marketing action on the part of the companies.

**Study 7: Consumer Survey—Market V.**

**Study 8: Consumer Panel—Market V.**

**Study 9: Distribution Panel—Market V.**

**Study 10: Semantic Scales—Market V.**

**Study 11: Market Forecast—Market V.**

These studies are the counterparts for Vodites of Studies 1 to 6, with the exception of the Perceptual Mapping of Brands' Similarities and Preferences which is not available for Market V. It is indeed expected that the number of Vodite brands will not be high enough in the course of the game to make a non-metric multidimensional scaling study feasible. When no Vodite brand is available on the market, Study 10 will only give the perception of ideal values on the semantic scales for each segment, and would be used primarily for R & D planning. In the same situation, Study 11 will give a forecast of the potential market for the next period if a Vodite brand were

---

[3] For a presentation of non-metric multidimensional techniques see, for example, P. E. Green and F. J. Carmone, *Multidimensional Scaling and Related Techniques in Marketing Analysis,* Boston, Mass.: Allyn and Bacon, 1970.

introduced, based on declared purchase intentions obtained from a sample of individuals. It should be noted that in this case the market forecast obviously does not rely on history and tends to be less accurate and generally somewhat optimistic. Studies 7, 8 and, 9 are irrelevant when no Vodite brand is available on the market, and their request would result in wasting the corresponding expenditure.

**Study 12: Competitive Advertising Estimates.** Estimates of the total advertising expenditures for each competitive brand are provided by an advertising research firm. These estimates are also given for the brands of the company requesting the study as a reference to control for estimation errors.

**Study 13: Competitive Sales Force Estimates.** Estimates of the sales force sizes of competitive companies and their breakdown by channel of distribution are obtained from a specialized market research firm. The same estimates are also given for the sales force of the company requesting the study as a reference to control for estimation errors.

**Study 14: Sales Force Experiment.** A sales force experiment is set up in regional test markets by increasing the number of salesmen per channel. The experimental results are then used to estimate the number of distributors and market share each of the company's brands would have had in the entire market if the sales force directed to each channel had been increased by 5 salesmen.

**Study 15: Advertising Experiment.** An advertising experiment is conducted, increasing the advertising budget in selected regional test markets. The experimental results are used to project what the level of brand awareness and the share of market would have been for each of the company brands in the total market if the advertising budget had been increased for that brand by ten percent over the actual expenditures. The estimates are also broken down by segment. The experiment tests only size of budget, not changes in other parts of advertising strategy.

### Positioning, Repositioning, and Segmentation

Each MARKSTRAT company starts with two Sonite brands. During the course of the game, it may introduce new Sonite or Vodite brands, and reposition or withdraw existing ones. The maximum number of brands marketed by one company in a given period is limited to five. The positioning and repositioning of brands with respect to the specific needs of various consumer segments is a major aspect of the MARKSTRAT companies' marketing strategy.

One basis for analyzing the respective positioning of competitive brands is the perceptual mapping of similarities and preferences obtained in Marketing Research Study 5, an example of which is shown in Exhibit 6. The example in Exhibit 6 is presented for explanatory purposes only and should not be used during the game, as it does not correspond to game conditions. The study provides a two-dimensional map, as this configuration was found statistically satisfactory. The interpretation of the two dimensions shown is not reported, although it will be in the actual study. Each axis is arbitrarily scaled from $-20$ to $+20$.

The numbers 1, 2, 3, 4, and 5 on the graph represent the positioning of the ideal points for each of the five segments. For instance, consumers from Segment 3 would globally most prefer a brand which would have coordinates at 16.3 on axis 1 and 7.5 on axis 2 of the perceptual map. The letters on the graph correspond to the positioning of the competitive brands on the market at the time of the study, as indicated in the bottom table of the exhibit. No significant difference was observed between the perception of the brands by the various segments. This means that although the segments prefer different ideal products, they perceive existing brands in a similar way. Thus, only one map for all segments is needed, rather than a separate map for each segment.

This map  graphically summarizes a great deal of information with regard to the relative perception of the various brands. As a first step, it indicates the relative competition which may be expected between the different brands. The prime competitors for brand SEMI (E) are expected to be, in decreasing order of importance: brands SULI (N), SELF (F), SIRU (J), SARE (D), and SONY (M). These brands are indeed perceived as being positioned closer to each other by consumers. The decreasing order of importance is determined by the straight-line distance between SEMI and the other brands' positions. On the other hand, little competition should be expected between brands SEMI (E) and SIRO (H), which are positioned far apart and should accordingly satisfy different needs. Cannibalism may also appear if a company's brands are positioned too close together; as, for instance, SIRO (H) and SIBI (I), which are both marketed by Company 3. The relative preference of a segment for different brands may also be inferred from the distance between the segment's ideal point and the positions of the brands. In our example, SIRO (H), SIBI (I), and SUSI (O) are principal competitors for Segment 5. SETA (G) is in a privileged situation with Segment 1, while  there are no brands positioned close to Segments 2's ideal point.

Using the information contained in such a perceptual map, a company may select between various strategic alternatives, such as specialization with respect to a specific segment or the simultaneous penetration of several segments with a given brand. Brands may be repositioned to achieve this. Repositioning can be affected by advertising or by research and development. Using advertising to reposition a product requires three types of decisions:

1. Specifying perceptual objectives for the brand. For instance, if one wants to reposition SEMI (E) closer to the ideal point of Segment 4, one could specify perceptual objectives of 15.5 on axis 1 and 4.8 on axis 2. This would serve as a guideline for the design of appropriate advertising platforms, copy, or media plans.

2. Allocating an advertising budget for the brand. The higher this budget, the further one may expect to be able to reposition the brand.

3. Allocating an advertising research budget is necessary for copy testing and media selection. The higher the advertising research budget, the more accurate one may expect to be in reaching the perceptual objectives.

EXHIBIT 6
Perceptual Mapping of Brands' Similarities and Preferences

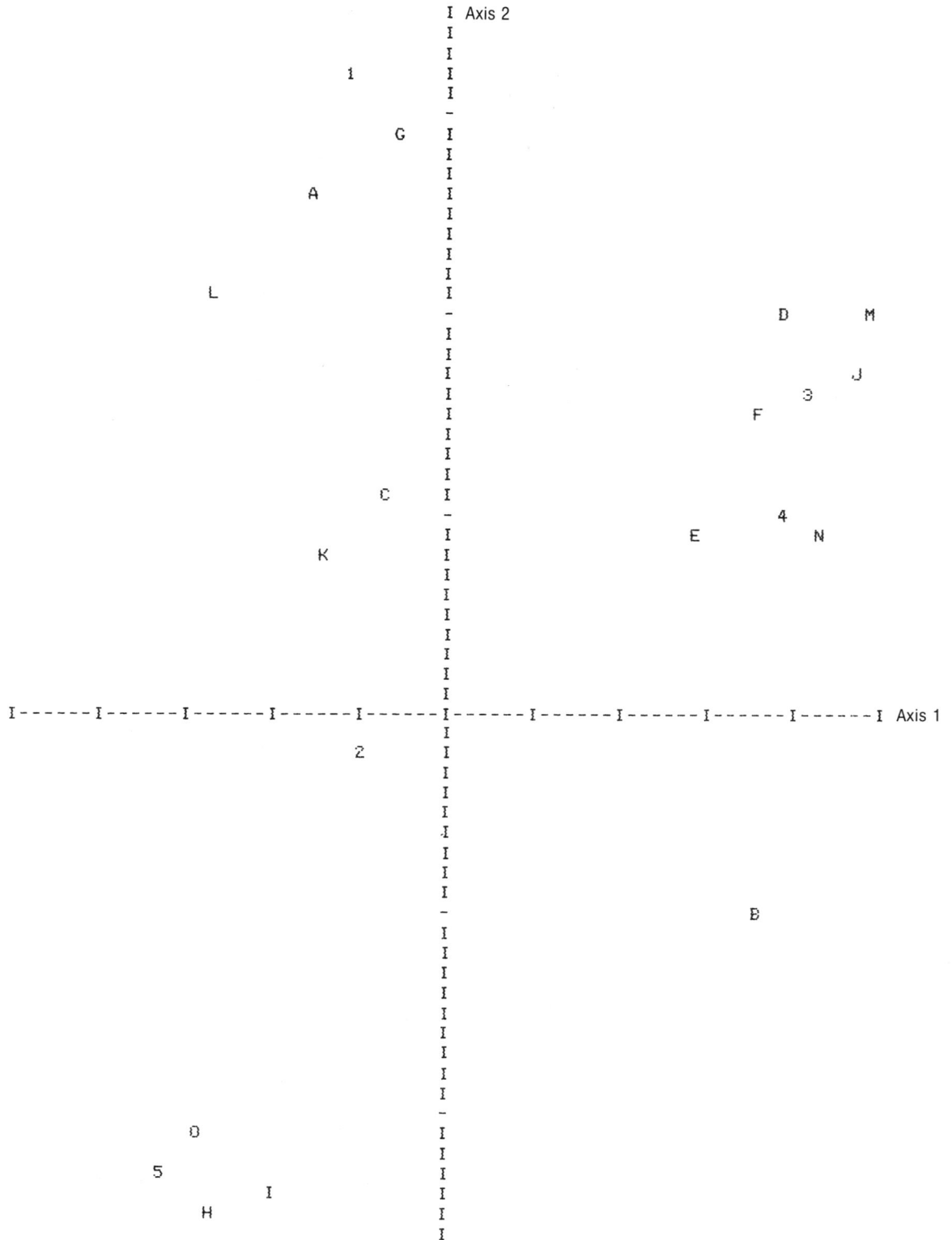

| IDEAL POINTS | * | SEGMENT | * | COORD.AXIS1 | * | COORD.AXIS2 | * |
|---|---|---|---|---|---|---|---|
| 1 | * | 1 | * | -4.4 | * | 15.8 | * |
| 2 | * | 2 | * | -4.2 | * | -1.0 | * |
| 3 | * | 3 | * | 16.3 | * | 7.5 | * |
| 4 | * | 4 | * | 15.5 | * | 4.8 | * |
| 5 | * | 5 | * | -13.2 | * | -11.9 | * |

| POSITIONING | * | BRAND | * | COORD.AXIS1 | * | COORD.AXIS2 | * | COMMENTS | * |
|---|---|---|---|---|---|---|---|---|---|
| A | * | SAMA | * | -6.1 | * | 12.8 | * | | |
| B | * | SALT | * | 14.5 | * | -5.0 | * | | |
| C | * | SALK | * | -3.0 | * | 5.5 | * | | |
| D | * | SARE | * | 15.5 | * | 10.0 | * | | |
| E | * | SEMI | * | 11.5 | * | 4.5 | * | | |
| F | * | SELF | * | 14.2 | * | 7.5 | * | | |
| G | * | SETA | * | -2.2 | * | 14.4 | * | | |
| H | * | SIRO | * | -11.0 | * | -12.8 | * | | |
| I | * | SIBI | * | -7.7 | * | -12.5 | * | | |
| J | * | SIRU | * | 18.6 | * | 8.1 | * | | |
| K | * | SOLD | * | -5.7 | * | 3.5 | * | | |
| L | * | SONO | * | -10.8 | * | 10.1 | * | | |
| M | * | SONY | * | 19.7 | * | 9.5 | * | | |
| N | * | SULI | * | 17.0 | * | 4.3 | * | | |
| O | * | SUSI | * | -11.5 | * | -10.5 | * | | |

Brand repositioning by advertising is limited, however, by the actual physical characteristics, and consumers' perceptions of these characteristics may be shifted only within a certain range by advertising. At some point, it becomes more profitable to reposition a brand by changing its physical characteristics than by advertising alone. This requires the successful completion of an R & D project, which results in a product with the desired new characteristics. The physical characteristics desirable in a new product can be inferred from the perceptual map after careful analysis. It is important to note, in particular, that the scales on the perceptual axes are arbitrary and different from units in which the physical characteristics of the products are expressed, and that the perception of the brands' characteristics by consumers may be distorted. When a product has been produced by R & D, the company may decide to launch it under a new brand name or to use it to modify an existing brand. In the latter case, the improved product will benefit from an existing level of brand awareness.

As described above, the perceptual mapping of similarities and preferences is an important tool for the design of positioning and repositioning strategies. It may, however, lead to inadequate decisions if used without taking other factors into account. One should note that various brands have different awareness levels. One brand may be positioned close to a segment's ideal point but draw few purchases from the consumers if it is unknown. In addition, it can be expected that the higher the awareness level of a brand, the more difficult it will be to reposition the brand. The five segments represent different volumes of potential sales and are at different stages of their development. Their needs evolve over time and so, too, do their ideal points. Although the perceptual map reproduces brand similarities and preferences satisfactorily, as expressed by a sample of individuals, it is certainly incomplete; other dimensions may enter into consumers' perceptions. Finally, the design of a marketing strategy should take into account the possible moves by competitors which may seriously affect the market situation in the coming periods.

The semantic scale ratings provided in Marketing Research Study 4 also give perceptual and preference information for Sonites. The semantic scale results are less accurate than those obtained through perceptual mapping because of the cruder methodology used, but they are substantially less expensive to purchase. For Vodites, only the semantic scale ratings are available (Marketing Research Study 10).

### Implementation of the Marketing Strategy

Once the competitive market structure has been analyzed and a positioning strategy has been selected, it must be expressed in terms of elements of the marketing mix, and requirements must be made known to other departments of the firm. New brands may be added to the company's line and others may be modified, depending on the pool of successful R & D projects accumulated in the past. A global advertising budget, the proportion of the budget allocated to advertising research, and a recommended retail price need to be set for each brand. Advertising can have an effect on the repositioning of a brand, as indicated previously, as well as on its level of awareness and on its acceptance by distribution channels. In particular, awareness of a brand is expected to decrease in the absence of advertising because consumers forget.

The size of the sales force and its allocation to each channel must be decided during each period. The number of salesmen assigned to a channel directly influences the distribution coverage of the company's brands. Distributors are known to favor brands that are well advertised and those that are gaining market share. As the various segments have different shopping habits, it is essential that the allocation of the sales force effort between the three distribution channels be in harmony with the positioning and segmentation strategy.

Instructions must also be given to the production and R & D departments concerning their operations in the following yearly period. Taking into account the forecasted level of sales and the quantities available in inventory, a production level for the year is given to the production department for each brand. To maximize contribution, a balance between stock-outs and excessive inventories must be sought. During the course of a year, the production department can adjust its output to accommodate changing sales requirements, but only within the limited range corresponding to plus or minus twenty percent of the requested production plan. If, for instance, total demand for a Sonite brand is 150,000 units, while the production plan is 100,000 units without any inventory at the start of the period, the production level will automatically be adjusted upwards to 120,000 units and lost sales will be reduced to 30,000 units. If total demand was 110,000 units, production would be able to adjust exactly to this level. On the other hand, if total demand was 60,000 units, the production level would automatically be adjusted downwards to 80,000 units, and excess inventory would be reduced to 20,000 units.

Exhibit 7 summarizes the marketing-R&D interface. Marketing requests

EXHIBIT 7
The Marketing - R & D Interface

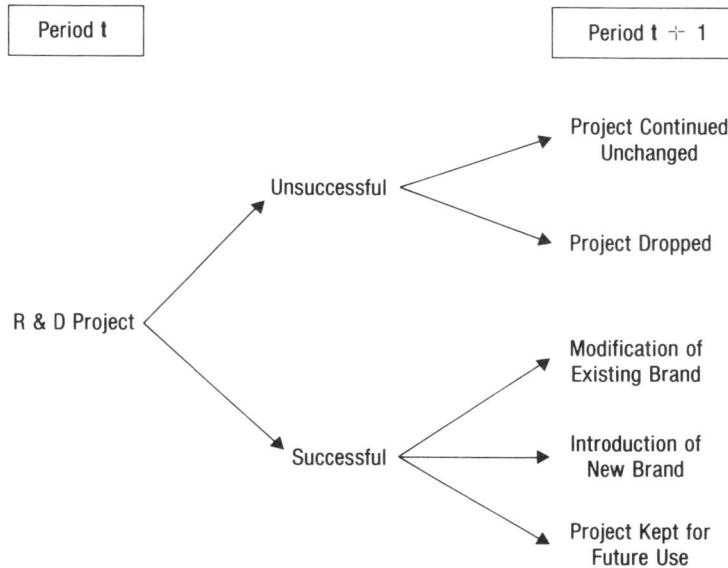

a project from the R&D department by specifying a project name, a budget, and the physical characteristics of the desired product. The Company Report for the following period will indicate whether the project has been successfully completed or not. If the desired product has not been found, the marketing department may ask R & D to pursue the project. In this case, it will have to invest additional funds in the project, without changing its name or characteristics. Only the cost characteristic of an ongoing project may be changed, particularly if inflation is to be taken into account. Alternatively, the project may be dropped, in which case the investment previously made is lost. Or, if one of the characteristics (except cost) of the desired product is changed, then a new project with a different name must be launched—without benefit from the investment previously made.

If the R&D project has successfully been completed, the marketing department may use the newly developed product to modify an existing brand or to introduce a new brand. The name of the project does not in any sense restrict the application of the new product. For instance, a new product developed through the R&D project "PSARO" may be used to modify the existing brand "SALT" or to launch a new brand named "SAFE." Alternatively, the firm may choose not to exploit the new product immediately, in which case it still remains available for use in future years.

It is important to note that it takes a minimum of one period, and sometimes several periods, between the launching of an R&D project and its possible use in the market place. Thus, the marketing-R&D interface requires particularly careful planning.

Among the various activities of the marketing department, four require the use of disposable funds within the limits set by the marketing budget: advertising, sales force, R&D, and marketing research. Trade-offs must obviously be made between these types of investments according to their relative impact on the company's objectives.

# 4

# Operating Instructions

Each of the five MARKSTRAT companies is managed by a team, and these five teams can organize themselves as they wish. It is, however, desirable that each team elect a chairman or a coordinator to facilitate communications with the game administrator. For each period, a deadline will be set for each team to submit a Decision Form representing their company's decisions for the current simulated year. The decisions for the five companies will then be used as inputs to the MARKSTRAT computerized simulation model. Each team will then receive the Company Report: a document containing their results for the period, general market information, and the marketing research studies they requested. The MARKSTRAT game will usually be played over six to ten simulated years.

To help the teams in the management of their companies, two additional documents are provided, the Budgeting Form and the Planning Form. The Budgeting Form is designed to facilitate computation of the estimated net marketing contribution in the next period, and the Planning Form is designed to appraise a company's performance over time. At the beginning of the game, each team receives the Company Report corresponding to Period 0 operations, which represents their company's initial situation. Thus, their first decisions deal with Period 1. These four documents (the Company Report, the Decision Form, the Budgeting Form, and the Planning Form) will now be described in detail.

# The Company Report

The printout of a sample Company Report is shown in Appendix A. It is given for descriptive purposes only, and the specific figures indicated should not be used in making decisions. It is made up of seven parts:

**1. General Results.** These show the performance of Firm 3 in Period 5 of a simulation. This firm has three brands on the market. The gross marketing contribution is computed for each of these brands as revenues less identifiable brand expenses (that is, costs of goods sold, inventory costs, and advertising expenditures). The average selling price used in the computation of revenues depends on the way brand sales are split among the three distribution channels, since channel margins are different. The unit transfer cost is the price that the marketing department is charged for the units sold. The marketing department is also charged for the inventory holding costs, because it is responsible for production volume. The inventory is valued at transfer prices and its holding costs are computed as a percentage of its value, according to the rate given in the Newsletter at the end of the Company Report. If the marketing department wants to drop a brand, the inventory of this brand will be written off as a total loss and charged to the marketing department at the transfer price. These costs will appear in the "extraordinary cost" account. When a brand is improved, the same procedure will apply to the inventory of the old product—in order to avoid having two products with the same brand names simultaneously available on the market. In these cases, the firm may negotiate with the game administrator the financial terms under which these obsolete stocks could be liquidated in markets external to the MARKSTRAT world. Revenues from the liquidation of these products will appear in the "extraordinary profit" account and will, partly at least, offset the incurred loss.

The expenditures that are not allocated by brands (that is, R & D, Sales Force, and Marketing Research costs) are then subtracted from gross marketing contribution to give the net marketing contribution. The budget available for the next period is a function of the net marketing contribution obtained. It is shown at the end of the General Results section. The Advertising, Sales Force, R & D, and Marketing Research expenditures for the next within this budget, although changes may be negotiated with the game administrator on the basis of a well-defined plan.

**2. Marketing.** For each of the company's brands, its market share and the number of distributors carrying the brand in each channel are given. The market share is computed on the basis of units sold. Finally, the number of salesmen allocated to each channel is indicated.

**3. Messages.** Messages are sometimes given to the companies, mainly when corrective action has been taken. For instance, if the assigned budget has been exceeded, arbitrary cuts in marketing expenditures will be indicated; if the price of a given brand is increased to such a level that market response is very unfavorable, downward adjustments are automatically performed and reported; if an R&D project that has not yet been completed is used to modify an existing brand or to launch a new one, the failure to implement the required actions will also be reported.

**4. R & D.** When a company has engaged in R & D projects, the cumulative expenditure made on each project is shown, as well as its current status. If the R & D project has been successfully completed, the value of the physical characteristics of the newly developed project are given. These correspond to the values originally requested. If the project has not been successfully completed, the R & D department will supply an estimate of the additional budget that it would need to bring the project to completion.

**5. Cumulative Results.** Cumulative results obtained by the company since Period 0 are presented in this section. The launching period of the brands available at the start of the simulation is indicated as Period 0, although they will generally have been introduced several years before. No R & D projects are in progress and no Marketing Research studies are available in Period 0.

**6. Newsletter.** The newsletter gives information that would normally be known to the industry at the end of the year. It first indicates the Gross National Product growth rate for the previous period and the forecasted rate for the next period, as well as the inflation rate for the previous period and the forecasted inflation rate for the next period. The new Sales Force, Marketing Research, and Inventory costs are given.

If new brands have been introduced on the market, or if existing brands have been modified, the values of their physical characteristics and their recommended retail prices are given. It is easy to recognize the origins of a brand from its name, the first letter indicating the product type and the second one identifying the company to which it belongs.

Information is then given on Markets S and V providing for each brand on the market: unit sales, market share based on units, recommended retail price, MMU sales, and market share based on the MMU sales.

**7. Marketing Research.** The Marketing Research studies requested by the company are presented following the newsletter.

# The Decision Form

A sample completed Decision Form is shown in Exhibit 8. It is the Decision Form of Firm 3 in Period 5, which resulted in the Company Report described previously. The industry number, the number of the current period, and the firm number; as well as the number of commercialized products, R&D projects, and Marketing Research studies desired by the company in the current period are entered at the top of the sheet. The industry number is used only when several MARKSTRAT simulations are run simultaneously, each with five different teams.

The Decision Form is then divided into four parts dealing with Product Management, Sales Force, R & D, and Marketing Research Studies. In the Product Management section, there may be up to five brands with their names indicated in the first column, according to the naming conventions previously described. If a modification is made to the physical characteristics of an existing brand, or if a new brand is introduced, the name of the R&D project that led to the improved or new product is indicated in the second column. If no modification to the brand is made in the current period, the second column is left blank. In the sample Decision Form the brand SIRU was developed through the R & D project PSIRA, whereas SIRO and SIBI are non-modified existing brands. In order to be able to modify or to introduce a brand in a given period, it is obviously required that the corresponding R&D project had been successfully completed in a previous period. A project requested from the R&D department is never available for commercialization before the beginning of the following period. The relevant R&D project name should be indicated only in the first period of a modification or of an introduction.

For each brand, the production level request, the advertising budget, the percentage of the advertising budget spent on advertising research, and the recommended retail price are indicated in the units specified at the top of the column. When trying to reposition a brand with advertising, perceptual objectives are given with numbers that correspond to the two axes of the perceptual map. These numbers should be between +20 and −20, the maximum and minimum coordinates of the axes. If the only data available for giving perceptual objectives come from semantic scales, some adjustments are required. First, the two dimensions that appear to be most important in the semantic scale study are assumed to correspond to axes 1 and 2 of the perceptual map, respectively. Second, the 1 to 7 semantic scales need to be transformed into coordinates from −20 to +20, as indicated in Exhibit 9. These will correspond to objectives in terms of the perceptual map. If no repositioning is desired or cannot be expressed in terms of the perceptual map

EXHIBIT 8
Sample Decision Form

# MARKSTRAT DECISION FORM

Firm _____ **3**

Name of Commercialized Product _____ **3**

Number of R & D Projects _____ **2**          Industry _____ **1**

Number of Marketing Research Studies **10**     Period _____ **5**

## PRODUCT MANAGEMENT

| Brand Names | Name of R & D Project (if modification or introduction) | Production Planning (thousand units) | Advertising Budget (thousands of $) | Advertising Research (percent) | Recommemded Retail Price ($) | Perceptual Objectives (−20 to +20, or 99) Axis 1 | Axis 2 |
|---|---|---|---|---|---|---|---|
| SIRO | — | 150 | 3000 | 5 | 600 | -13 | -12 |
| SIBI | — | 0 | 3000 | 5 | 1200 | 99 | 99 |
| SIRU | PSIRA | 200 | 7000 | 8 | 2600 | 12 | 5 |
|  |  |  |  |  |  |  |  |
|  |  |  |  |  |  |  |  |

## SALES FORCE

| Distribution Channels | 1 | 2 | 3 |
|---|---|---|---|
| Number of Salesmen | 30 | 40 | 30 |

## RESEARCH AND DEVELOPMENT

| Project Name | Expenditures (thousands of $) | Physical Characteristics 1 | 2 | 3 | 4 | 5 | 6 |
|---|---|---|---|---|---|---|---|
| PSIBO | 100 | 11 | 9 | 35 | 25 | 35 | 400 |
| PSICA | 200 | 10 | 8 | 35 | 30 | 50 | 500 |
|  |  |  |  |  |  |  |  |
|  |  |  |  |  |  |  |  |

## MARKET RESEARCH STUDIES

| 1 | 2 | 3 | 4 | 5 | 6 | 12 | 13 | 14 | 15 |  |  |  |
|---|---|---|---|---|---|---|---|---|---|---|---|---|

(for instructor's use)

|  |
|---|
|  |

ec(−)      ep(+)      bd(−)      bi(+)

EXHIBIT 8 (continued)
Sample Decision Form

## Modifications Resulting from Negotiations
## between the Firm and the Game Administrator

| Source of modification | Exceptional profit (+) or cost (−) (thoudands of $) | Budget increase (+) or decrease (−) (thousands of $) |
|---|---|---|
| 1. Additional information bought from the game administrator | | |
| STUDY #3 | −150 | −150 |
| CONSULTING ON SALES FORECAST FOR NEW PRODUCT | −200 | −200 |
| 2. Inventory liquidations compensated by the game administrator | | |
| Brand: | | |
| Brand: | | |
| 3. Changes in the budget | | +7350 |
| 4. Fines | | |
| 5. Other modifications | | |
| | | |
| | | |
| | | |
| Total | −350 | +7000 |

Signature of the firm's representative  _C. Smith_

Signature of the game administrator  _Mr. Jones_

EXHIBIT 9
Specification of Perceptual Objectives
from Semantic Scales Data

The semantic scales are defined on an interval from 1 to 7, while the perceptual objectives are defined in terms of coordinates on the perceptual map and can, thus, take values between $-20$ and $+20$:

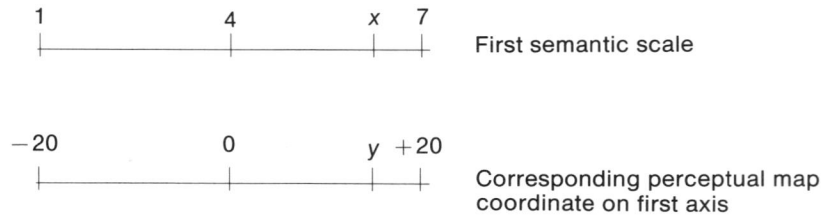

```
1             4         x  7
|-------------|---------|--+    First semantic scale


-20           0         y +20
|-------------|---------|--+    Corresponding perceptual map
                               coordinate on first axis
```

An interval of one unit on the semantic scale may be interpreted as 40/6 or 20/3 units on the axis of the perceptual map.

If only semantic scales data are available, and if value $x$ on a semantic scale is set as an objective in the repositioning of a given brand, the corresponding perceptual objective expressed in terms of a coordinate $y$ in the perceptual map may be computed with the following formula:

$$y = \frac{20}{3}(x - 4)$$

with $y$ as the value to be used as a perceptual objective in filling in the Decision Form. This transformation is obviously crude, but the use of numbers should not hide the intrinsic qualitative nature of perceptual objectives.

*Example*: If a given brand is to be repositioned towards value 6 on the first semantic scale, the perceptual objective to be entered on the Decision Form for axis 1 is :

$$y = \frac{20}{3}(6 - 4) = 13.3$$

axes because of a lack of data, the number 99 should be entered, as in the case of SIBI on the sample Decision Form. These perceptual objectives convey information primarily of a qualitative nature (for example, how much should the lightness of the product be stressed) for the design of the advertising platform and copy, as well as for the selection of media. The numeric representation of these perceptual objectives is used only for communication purposes.

In the next section of the Decision Form, the number of salesmen allocated to each channel of distribution is specified. The current costs of maintaining, hiring, or firing salesmen are indicated in the Newsletter of the Company Report.

In the third section of the Decision Form, up to four R & D projects may be specified in one period. Names should be given to R & D projects according to the convention previously described. There is no need for the name of an R & D project to correspond to the name of an existing or planned brand, although all current and past R & D projects must have different names. On the sample Decision Form, Firm 3 requests two R & D projects, both of which concerned with Sonite products. For each project, the amount to be spent in the current period, as well as the values of physical characteristics for the desired products, should be indicated. In particular, the feasible ranges of these characteristics for Sonites and Vodites, as indicated in Exhibit 3, should be noted.

In the last section, Marketing Research studies may be requested by specifying the number of each desired study on the bottom line of the Decision Form. The rectangle in the bottom right hand corner should be left blank for the game administrator's use. Finally, the back of the Decision Form should contain any modifications to the standard procedure resulting from a negotiation between the firm and the game administrator. These modifications may be due to the purchase of additional information from the game administrator, liquidation of obsolete inventories, or changes of budgets based on a well defined plan. In addition, fines may be imposed on a firm for delayed decisions, espionage, or inter-firm concerted actions. Each of these modifications may be expressed in terms of an exceptional profit, an exceptional cost, a budget increase, or a budget decrease. It is essential that this document be agreed upon and signed by the game administrator and a firm's representative.

# The Budgeting Form

The objective of the Budgeting Form represented in Exhibit 10 is to help to systematically specify the company's use of its marketing budget (extreme right-hand column) and estimate the net marketing contribution that may result from selected actions in the current period. It has the same structure as the first section of the Company Report and allows checking *a posteriori* for variations between a selected annual plan and the actual outcome. The crucial estimate in the budgeting process concerns, obviously, the forecasted sales for each brand. The table on the back of the Budgeting Form should help formulate these forecasts in terms of market sizes and market shares in each segment. The computations to be performed in the budgeting process are straight forward, with the possible exception of the average selling price. In computing the average selling price for a brand one has to take into account the recommended retail price, the expected allocation of the brand sales between distribution channels, and the margins practiced by each channel. This is essentially an internal Marketing Department Form, and is not submitted to the administrator.

EXHIBIT 10
Sample Budgeting Form

Firm _1_
Industry _3_
Period _5_

## MARKSTRAT BUDGETING FORM

| | | | |
|---|---|---|---|
| Brand Name | SIRO | SIBI | SIRU |
| Production (units) | 150 | 0 | 200 |
| Quantity Sold (units) | 180 | 100 | 230 |
| Inventory (units) | 0 | 400 | 0 |
| Retail Price ($) | 600 | 1,200 | 2,600 |
| Average Selling Price ($) | 370 | 740 | 1,620 |
| Unit Transfer Cost | 160 | 310 | 900 |
| Revenues (thousands of $) | 66,000 | 74,000 | 372,600 |
| Cost of Goods Sold (thousands of $) | 26,800 | 31,000 | 207,000 |
| Inventory Costs (thousands of $) | 0 | 14,260 | 0 |
| Advertising (thousands of $) | 3,000 | 3,000 | 7,000 |
| Gross Marketing Contribution (thousands of $) | 34,800 | 25,740 | 158,600 |

219,140

R & D (thousands of $) ......... 1,200
Sales Force (thousands of $) ......... 3,400
Marketing Research (thousands of $) ......... 700
Exceptional Cost or Profit (thousands of $) ......... 0
Net Marketing Contribution (thousands of $) ......... 213,840

13,000 Advertising
1,200 R & D
3,400 Sales Force
700 Marketing Research

18,300 Total Marketing Expenditures

Total Marketing Expenditures (thousands of $) .........

EXHIBIT 10 (continued)
Sample Budgeting Form

**Sales Forecast Input for Budgeting**

| | Total Sonite Market (thousands of units) | Total Vodite Market (thousands of units) | BRANDS — Market Share (on units), Sales (thousands of units) SIRO | SIBI | SIRU | | |
|---|---|---|---|---|---|---|---|
| Segment 1 | 110 | | 5 \| 6 | 5 \| 6 | 3 \| 3 | --- | --- |
| Segment 2 | 230 | | 20 \| 46 | 15 \| 35 | 4 \| 9 | --- | --- |
| Segment 3 | 600 | | 1 \| 6 | 0 \| 0 | 20 \| 120 | --- | --- |
| Segment 4 | 900 | | 1 \| 9 | 0 \| 0 | 11 \| 99 | --- | --- |
| Segment 5 | 250 | | 45 \| 110 | 25 \| 63 | 0 \| 0 | --- | --- |
| Aggregate Forecasts | 2,090 | | 65 \| 178 | 5 \| 104 | 11 \| 231 | --- | --- |

# The Planning Form

The Planning Form in Exhibit 11 is designed to formalize quantifiable objectives and to provide a basis for the appraisal of a company's performance over successive simulated years of the MARKSTRAT game. Three performance criteria are specified, as well as the four major types of expenditure under the direct control of the Marketing department. Some room is left in order to specify other items that are considered relevant in the evaluation of the firm's performance. On the back of the Planning Form, the firm should specify the main strategic options on which the formulated plan is based. This Form should be analyzed and updated each period according to the company's evolution. Although this form is primarily for internal use, it may be requested at any time by the game administrator in his negotiations with the firm. Finally, the successive plans realized in the course of the simulation will help the firm to evaluate and present its activities at the end of the game. Since each company starts in a different initial situation, it is not possible to directly compare the results of the five firms. It is, however, interesting to compare their different approaches in the light of their specific characteristics and to evaluate their respective successes and failures.

EXHIBIT 11
Sample Planning Form

## MARKSTRAT PLANNING FORM

Firm _____
Industry _____

### GENERAL PERFORMANCE

| | | PERIODS | | | | | | | | | |
|---|---|---|---|---|---|---|---|---|---|---|---|
| | | 1 | 2 | 3 | 4 | 5 | 6 | 7 | 8 | 9 | 10 |
| Turnover (millions of $) | Objective | 50 | 80 | 110 | 110 | 500 | 600 | 800 | 1,000 | 4,200 | 15,000 |
| | Outcome | 52 | 98 | 97 | 73 | | | | | | |
| Market Share (percent, on turnover) | Objective | 15 | 15 | 18 | 9 | 15 | 17 | 20 | 22 | 22 | 22 |
| | Outcome | 14 | 15 | 9 | 4 | | | | | | |
| Net Marketing Contribution (millions of $) | Objective | 6 | 40 | 60 | 50 | 210 | 250 | 350 | 500 | 600 | 800 |
| | Outcome | 5 | 53 | 35 | 26 | | | | | | |

### MARKETING EXPENDITURES

| | | 1 | 2 | 3 | 4 | 5 | 6 | 7 | 8 | 9 | 10 |
|---|---|---|---|---|---|---|---|---|---|---|---|
| Advertising (millions of $) | Objective | 5.2 | 4.5 | 4.1 | 0 | 13.0 | 18.0 | 26.0 | 34.0 | 42.0 | 49.0 |
| | Outcome | 5.2 | 4.5 | 4.1 | 0 | | | | ~ | | |
| Sales Force (millions of $) | Objective | 1.4 | 1.85 | 1.55 | 2.9 | 3.4 | 4.0 | 5.0 | 7.0 | 10.0 | 12.0 |
| | Outcome | 1.4 | 1.85 | 1.55 | 2.9 | | | | | | |
| R & D (millions of $) | Objective | 0 | 0.8 | 0.46 | 4.12 | 1.2 | 4.0 | 5.0 | 6.0 | 7.0 | 8.0 |
| | Outcome | 0 | 0.8 | 0.46 | 4.12 | | | | | | |
| Marketing Research (millions of $) | Objective | 0 | 0 | 0 | 0 | 0.7 | 0.8 | 0.9 | 1.1 | 1.3 | 1.5 |
| | Outcome | 0 | 0 | 0 | 0 | | | | | | |
| Total Marketing Expenditures (millions of $) | Objective | 6.6 | 7.15 | 6.11 | 7.02 | 18.3 | 26.8 | 36.9 | 48.1 | 60.3 | 70.5 |
| | Outcome | 6.6 | 7.15 | 6.11 | 7.02 | 18.3 | | | | | |

### OTHERS

| | | | | | | | | | | | |
|---|---|---|---|---|---|---|---|---|---|---|---|
| | Objectives | | | | | | | | | | |
| | Outcome | | | | | | | | | | |
| | Objective | | | | | | | | | | |
| | Outcome | | | | | | | | | | |

EXHIBIT 11 (continued)
Sample Planning Form

**Main Strategic Options**

Markets and Segments *DO NOT ENTER VODITE MARKET, CONCENTRATE ON SELECTED SEGMENTS. SEGMENT 5 → DOMINATE & MILK SEGMENTS 3/4 → STRONG ENTRY (GROWTH).*

Competition *EXPECTED TO DIVERT RESOURCES IN VODITES. LOCKED OUT OF SEGMENT 5. VULNERABLE IN SEGMENTS 3/4.*

Brands *SMALL NUMBER OF BRANDS. IN LONGER TERM, DEVELOP BRANDS IN SEGMENTS 3/4 TO CONSOLIDATE, WHILE PROTECTING SIRO & SIBI.*

Advertising *PROGRESSIVELY DECREASE ON SIRO & SIBI. CONCENTRATE ON GROWING MARKET (SIRU).*

Sales Force and Distribution *FOLLOW COMPETITION. IF SIRU RECEIVED BETTER IN SEGMENT 4 THAN SEGMENT 3, CONCENTRATE ON CHANNELS 1 & 2.*

Research & Developmemt *IMPROVE SIBI — GET RID OF EXCESS INVENTORY. PREPARE PRODUCTS FOR SEGMENT 4.*

Marketing Research *SYSTEMATICALLY FOLLOW SONITE MARKET ONLY.*

Economic Environment *REDUCTION IN PRODUCTION COSTS & MARKET MATURATION MAY CREATE PRICE WAR & INDUSTRY SHAKE-OUT. RAISING INFLATION MAY BRING PRICE CONTROLS.*

Others

# 5
# Final Considerations

You are now ready to participate in the MARKSTRAT simulation. You certainly have not yet assimilated all the information contained in this manual, and the main purpose of the first period decisions will be to familiarize yourself with the MARKSTRAT world and the mechanics of the game. After having been assigned to a firm, you will receive the Company Report of your firm for Period 0 from the game administrator. You will notice that each firm markets two brands with different market shares, and you will be able to evaluate the relative market strength of your firm compared to the competition. You will have no marketing research information at this stage, and you should not take inconsiderate risks. In particular, you will not be able to specify perceptual objectives in the absence of semantic scale or perceptual data, and you should write in the code 99 in the corresponding columns of the Decision Form. Likewise, you should not undertake R&D projects before having a better understanding of market needs, and you will obviously not be able to modify brands or to introduce new ones, as your firm has not yet completed any R&D projects.

You will, thus, concentrate on the management of your two existing brands and your sales force. In the process of reaching your decisions for Period 1, you should analyze the actions of your firm's previous management team in Period 0. It is not wise, at this stage, to drastically change their advertising, pricing, sales force, and production policies. On the other hand, you may consider purchasing Marketing Research studies, which will be made available for your next set of decisions in Period 2.

Exhibits 12 and 13 recapitulate the conventions for brand and R&D project names, as well as general background information that is given in various parts of this manual. You should note that the Exhibits in the text summarize critical information, and that they can be referred to easily through the table of contents.

During the first sets of decisions, it is essential that you rapidly develop good working relationships in your group. In particular, each member of your group should be involved in the discussion of all issues and should develop a grasp of the total situation. Later in the simulation—when everybody will have a common understanding of the strategic issues and the management of the firm will become more complex in terms of the number of brands, the R&D interface, the market developments, and the intensity of competition—some specific problem areas can be delegated to individuals. In this way, the group should learn to work efficiently, and each of its members should benefit equally from the MARKSTRAT experience.

EXTIBIT 12
Conventions for Brand and R & D Project Names


*Brand Names*

· Brand names consist of four letters
· The first letter is "S" for a Sonite product and "V" for a Vodite produrt
· The second letter identifies the company in the following way:

| Second letter | Firm number |
|:---:|:---:|
| A | 1 |
| E | 2 |
| I | 3 |
| O | 4 |
| U | 5 |

· The last two letters may be freely chosen by a company when launching a new brand, *as long as all brands have different names.*

*R & D Project Names*

· R & D project names consist of five letters
· The first letter is always "P"
· The second letter identifies the type of product that is being searched for: "S" for Sonites and "V" for Vodites
· The last three letters may be freely chosen by a company, *as long as its projects (current and past) have different names*
· The R & D project name bears no relationship to the commercialized brand name. Thus, "PSUZZ" may be used to improve existing brand "SULI" or to create a new brand "SUZI"

EXHIBIT 13
General Background Information

1. Average annual inflation rate over last 3 years: 9%

2. Average annual price increases in the Sonite market over the last 3 years: 10%

3. Percent of Sonite unit sales by segment in the last year:

> Segment 1: 30%
> Segment 2: 15%
> Segment 3: 20%
> Segment 4: 16%
> Segment 5: 19%

4. Average annual increases of Sonite unit sales over the last 3 years:

> Total: 35%
>
> Segment 1: 05%
> Segment 2: 25%
> Segment3: 50%
> Segment 4: 60%
> Segment 5: 30%

5. Total number of potential distributors of Sonites or Vodites:

> Channel 1:  3,000
> Channel 2: 35,000
> Channel 3:  4,000

6. Average margins of distributors as a percentage of retail price:

> Channel 1: 40%
> Channel 2: 35%
> Channel 3: 40%

7. Average advertising expenditures as a percentage of sales over the last 3 years: 10%

8. Average advertising research expenditures as a percentage of total advertising expenditures over the last 3 years: 5%

In previous administrations of the MARKSTRAT simulation, it has also been found that you will gain more from the learning experience by following the following advice:

*Emphasis on strategic issues.* Concentrate your efforts on strategic issues and long-term planning. The simulation purposely does not consider short-term activities such as promotions or the design of advertising research studies. In addition, some adjustments are automatically performed within a simulated period to relieve the burden of some operational problems, such as production planning.

*Importance of analysis.* Before making decisions, be sure that you understand the behavior of the market. Do not jump to the first explanation, or conclusion, that you may have reached when faced with a problem—it may be incomplete. Be careful that at various points in the simulation, as the caution about railroad crossings has it: "one train may hide another one." The detailed analysis of Marketing Research studies, of your own situation and of past competitive behavior, should help you reach more robust decisions.

*Group time allocation.* Make sure that you allocate your discussion time sensibly between problem areas. You will be under pressure to return your Decision Form by a given deadline, and you should avoid making decisions hastily in the last minutes available. Do not waste time on the discussion of a $100,000 issue if it will force you to rush through other decisions where millions of MMUs are at stake.

*Administrative errors.* Your team will have to bear the consequence of administrative errors made in filling out the Decision Form, and they cannot be corrected retroactively. In particular, be careful to express your production plan and your advertising budget in the specified units.

*Artificial accuracy.* Avoid artificial accuracy in quantifying your decisions. For instance, a specified advertising budget of 3,115 thousand MMUs will certainly not have an impact much different than a budget of 3,100, or even 3,000, thousand MMUs. This artificial accuracy may only give you a feeling of false confidence; or draw your attention too much toward the numbers themselves, while the main issues are in the strategic options that lie behind the numbers.

*Role of the game administrator.* The game administrator does not manipulate the simulation parameters in the course of the game. The MARKSTRAT simulation has been designed to automatically generate environmental changes. The markets will evolve mainly according to the actions taken by the competing firms. There will, thus, be no interference by the game administrator in favor of or against any firm, and you should feel entirely responsible for your firm's performance. The game administrator will play several roles, such as: consultant, to help you to solve some specific problems or to give you his personal opinion on some issues; marketing research firm, to sell you, at a premium price, some studies that you forgot to request on your Decision Form; chief executive officer of your firm, to negotiate your proposals for budget modifications; export firm, to help you liquidate obsolete inventories. In addition, he will also play the role of a justice court for espionage cases or for any complaint submitted by the firm. On the whole, you will find your game administrator quite resourceful. You may have to pay for some of his services, but all competitors will be treated equally. You will, however, find yourself in a better negotiating position if you can produce well-documented evidence for your requests.

In the final analysis, even though extensive marketing information is available to you that will allow you to systematically analyze market situations, you will soon realize that your judgement will have to play an important role in making your decisions. As in most real cases, there is no single specific solution to any of the problems that you will encounter. There are, however, alternatives that will clearly appear inferior after good analysis of the situation. There are other alternatives that will appear satisfactory but for which the relative merits depend mainly on the uncertainties of competitive actions. You will have, in this case, to use your judgement of competitive behavior and to make choices under uncertainty. Over a series of decisions, sound analysis and good judgement will inevitably bear fruit.

We hope that participating in the MARKSTRAT simulation will give you a better understanding of marketing strategy concepts, and that you will enjoy this learning experience. We wish you success in the management of your firm.

# Appendix A

# Sample Company Report

The following represents the sample Company Report of Firm 3 in Period 5 of a MARKSTRAT simulation. The decision of Firm 3 for the same period are specified in Exhibit 8. This is only an example, the data that it contains should not be used in making your decisions.

```
          COMPANY REPORT      FIRM 3            PERIOD   5


   1 - GENERAL RESULTS
       ---------------
     (IN THOUSANDS $ EXCEPT WHEN INDICATED)


              *****************************
   BRANDS     *  SIRO  *  SIBI  *  SIRU  *
              *****************************
   PRODUCTION *  168602*       0*  160000*UNITS
   UNITS SOLD *  168602*   74648*  127699*UNITS
   INVENTORY  *       0*  398461*   32301*UNITS
              *        *        *        *
   RETAIL PRICE*    600*    1200*    2600* $
   AV.SEL.PRICE*    370*     741*    1611* $
   UNIT TR.COST*    152*     346*    2483* $
              *        *        *        *
   REVENUES   *   62303*   55321*  205759*
   COST OF G.S.*  25651*   25809*  317078*
   INV.HLD.COST*      0*   17220*   10025*
              *****************************
   ADVERTISING *   3000*    3000*    7000*
              *        *        *        *
   GROSS MKTG. *        *        *        *
   CONTRIBUTION*   33652*    9293* -128345*   -85400
              *****************************
   R & D...................................      1200
   SALES FORCE.............................      3444
   MARKETING RESEARCH......................       660
   EXCEPTIONAL
   COST OR PROFIT..........................         0
   NET MARKETING
   CONTRIBUTION............................    -90705

   NEXT PERIOD BUDGET............    7000



   2 - MARKETING
       ---------


              *****************************
   BRANDS     *  SIRO  *  SIBI  *  SIRU  *
              *****************************
   MARKET SHARE*   0.07*    0.03*    0.06*
   (ON UNITS) *****************************



   NUMBER OF
   DISTRIBUTORS
              *****************************
   CHANNEL 1  *    1079*     955*    1148*
              *        *        *        *
   CHANNEL 2  *   14603*   13055*   15605*
              *        *        *        *
   CHANNEL 3  *    1439*    1273*    1531*
              *****************************



   SALES FORCE
            CHANNEL1 CHANNEL2 CHANNEL3
            *****************************
            *   30   *   40   *   30   *
            *****************************
```

3 - MESSAGES
    -------


4 - R & D
    -----

```
                    ***********************
PROJECTS            *  PSIBO  *  PSICA  *
                    *         *         *
CUMUL. EXPENDITURES* 1000000* 200000*
                    *         *         *
                    ***********************
                    *         *         *
PROJECT SUCCESSFUL  *    YES*      NO  *
*****************************************
*           *   1   *     11*      10*
*           *   2   *      9*       8*
*CHARACTE-  *   3   *    350*     350*
* RISTICS   *   4   *     25*      30*
*           *   5   *     35*      50*
*           *   6   *    400*     500*
*****************************************
```

ADDITIONAL BUDGET REQUESTED BY R&D TO COMPLETE PSICA : 1300000


5 - CUMULATIVE RESULTS ( IN THOUSAND $ )
    ------------------------------------

|  |  |  |  | CUMULATIVE |
| BRAND | LAUNCHING PERIOD | UNITS SOLD | ADVERTISING | GROSS MKTG. CONTRIBUTION |
| ------ | --------- | ------ | --------- | ----------- |
| SIRO | 0 | 426 | 17200 | 84468 |
| SIBI | 0 | 442 | 15800 | 87737 |
| SIRU | 5 | 128 | 7000 | -128345 |

TOTAL CUMULATIVE RETAIL SALES................    1144127

TOTAL CUMULATIVE ADVERTISING................      40000

TOTAL CUMULATIVE GROSS MARKETING CONTRIB....      43861

TOTAL CUMULATIVE R&D EXPENDITURES..........       5550

TOTAL CUMULATIVE SALES FORCE EXPENDITURES...     11757

TOTAL CUMULATIVE MARKET RESEARCH EXPEND.....      1615

TOTAL CUMULATIVE NET MARKETING CONTRIBUTION.    -68043

```
6 - NEWSLETTER
--------------
        (ALL MONEY AMOUNTS IN $ )


          - G N P GROWTH RATE THIS PERIOD= .05

          - ESTIMATED GNP GROWTH RATE NEXT PERIOD= .07

          - INFLATION RATE THIS PERIOD= .11

          - ESTIMATED INFLATION RATE NEXT PERIOD= .13

          - COST OF A SALESMAN NEXT PERIOD= 38300.

          - COST OF FIRING A SALESMAN NEXT PERIOD = 9200

          - COST OF TRAINING A NEW SALESMAN NEXT PERIOD = 5300

          - COST OF MARKETING RESEARCH STUDIES NEXT PERIOD :

# 1=115000       # 2=192400       # 3=115000       # 4= 18800       # 5= 67100
# 6= 38300       # 7= 76800       # 8=134600       # 9= 96000       #10= 18800
#11= 38300       #12= 57200       #13= 28300       #14= 45800       #15= 67100



        - INVENTORY HOLDING COST PER ANNUM=  12.5           %
              ( % OF TRANSFER COST )



        - NEW BRANDS OR PRODUCT MODIFICATIONS INTRODUCED
                 OVER THE LAST PERIOD

  *******************************************************************
  *         *          P H Y S I C A L              *  RETAIL  *
  *BRANDS  *   C H A R A C T E R I S T I C S         *  PRICE   *
  *         *  ***************************************  *         *
  *         *  1  *  2  *  3  *  4  *  5  *  6  *         *
  *******************************************************************
  *  SAMA  *  17  * 10  * 500 *  25 * 100 * 1000 *  1300.00 *
  *  SALK  *  12  *  9  * 400 *  25 *  65 *  650 *  1400.00 *
  *  SARE  *  15  *  8  * 500 *  20 * 100 *  600 *  2100.00 *
  *  VELD  * 100  * 15  *  40 *  10 *  30 *  400 *  1200.00 *
  *  SIRU  *  15  *  9  * 500 *  30 *  80 * 1000 *  2600.00 *
  *******************************************************************
```

- INFORMATION ON MARKET S

| BRANDS | * | UNIT SALES | * | MARKET SHARE (UNITS) | * | RETAIL PRICE | * | $ SALES | * | MARKET SHARE ($ SALES) | * |
|--------|---|-----------|---|---------------------|---|-------------|---|---------|---|-----------------------|---|
| SAMA | * | 41285* | 0.02 | * | 1300.00* | | 53670503* | | 0.01 | * |
| SALT | * | 31959* | 0.01 | * | 1900.00* | | 60722103* | | 0.01 | * |
| SALK | * | 36186* | 0.02 | * | 1400.00* | | 50660399* | | 0.01 | * |
| SARE | * | 222092* | 0.10 | * | 2100.00* | | 466393207* | | 0.10 | * |
| SEMI | * | 498400* | 0.22 | * | 1950.00* | | 971880043* | | 0.21 | * |
| SELF | * | 187595* | 0.08 | * | 2450.00* | | 459607733* | | 0.10 | * |
| SETA | * | 8147* | 0.00 | * | 1500.00* | | 12220500* | | 0.00 | * |
| SIRO | * | 168602* | 0.07 | * | 600.00* | | 101161198* | | 0.02 | * |
| SIBI | * | 74648* | 0.03 | * | 1200.00* | | 89577598* | | 0.02 | * |
| SIRU | * | 127699* | 0.06 | * | 2600.00* | | 332017401* | | 0.07 | * |
| SOLD | * | 105306* | 0.05 | * | 1400.00* | | 147428413* | | 0.03 | * |
| SONO | * | 23016* | 0.01 | * | 900.00* | | 20714400* | | 0.00 | * |
| SONY | * | 87637* | 0.04 | * | 2500.00* | | 219092507* | | 0.05 | * |
| SULI | * | 649246* | 0.28 | * | 2400.00* | | 1558190305* | | 0.34 | * |
| SUSI | * | 20810* | 0.01 | * | 600.00* | | 12486000* | | 0.00 | * |
| TOTAL | | 2282628 | 1.00 | | | | 4555821978 | | 1.00 | |

AVERAGE PRICE= $ 1995.87

- INFORMATION ON MARKET V

| BRANDS | * | UNIT SALES | * | SHARE (UNITS) | * | RETAIL PRICE | * | $ SALES | * | SHARE ($ SALES) | * |
|--------|---|-----------|---|--------------|---|-------------|---|---------|---|----------------|---|
| VERA | * | 7913* | 0.22 | * | 690.00* | | 5459970* | | 0.23 | * |
| VELO | * | 4498* | 0.13 | * | 1200.00* | | 5397600* | | 0.23 | * |
| VUME | * | 23299* | 0.65 | * | 560.00* | | 13047440* | | 0.55 | * |
| TOTAL | | 35710 | 1.00 | | | | 23905012 | | 1.00 | |

AVERAGE PRICE= $ 669.42

# Appendix B

# Sample Marketing Research Studies

The following printouts contain the Marketing Research Studies requested by Firm 3 in Period 5 of a MARKSTRAT simulation, as indicated in the Sample Decision Form in Exhibit 8. This is only an example, the data that it contains should not be used in making your decisions.

STUDY 1: CONSUMER SURVEY - MARKET S
-------------------------------------

**BRAND AWARENESS (NO SIGNIFICANT DIFFERENCES OBSERVED BETWEEN SEGMENTS)

| | | | |
|---|---|---|---|
| SAMA 0.572 | SALT 0.349 | SALK 0.303 | SARE 0.542 |
| SEMI 0.662 | SELF 0.625 | SETA 0.139 | |
| SIRO 0.563 | SIBI 0.573 | SIRU 0.374 | |
| SOLD 0.523 | SONO 0.508 | SONY 0.387 | |
| SULI 0.458 | SUSI 0.443 | | |

**PURCHASE INTENTS

| | SEGMENT 1 | SEGMENT 2 | SEGMENT 3 | SEGMENT 4 | SEGMENT 5 | TOTAL |
|---|---|---|---|---|---|---|
| SAMA | 0.325 | 0.058 | 0.007 | 0.007 | 0.015 | 0.032 |
| SALT | 0.015 | 0.017 | 0.018 | 0.027 | 0.006 | 0.019 |
| SALK | 0.088 | 0.104 | 0.005 | 0.006 | 0.012 | 0.023 |
| SARE | 0.039 | 0.019 | 0.144 | 0.119 | 0.006 | 0.093 |
| SEMI | 0.058 | 0.041 | 0.141 | 0.294 | 0.011 | 0.165 |
| SELF | 0.047 | 0.025 | 0.153 | 0.102 | 0.008 | 0.090 |
| SETA | 0.058 | 0.009 | 0.002 | 0.002 | 0.003 | 0.006 |
| SIRO | 0.025 | 0.083 | 0.004 | 0.004 | 0.608 | 0.107 |
| SIBI | 0.028 | 0.116 | 0.004 | 0.005 | 0.219 | 0.052 |
| SIRU | 0.020 | 0.011 | 0.083 | 0.071 | 0.004 | 0.054 |
| SOLD | 0.133 | 0.414 | 0.007 | 0.008 | 0.032 | 0.066 |
| SONO | 0.101 | 0.038 | 0.004 | 0.004 | 0.015 | 0.015 |
| SONY | 0.019 | 0.010 | 0.066 | 0.051 | 0.004 | 0.041 |
| SULI | 0.026 | 0.017 | 0.359 | 0.297 | 0.006 | 0.222 |
| SUSI | 0.020 | 0.040 | 0.003 | 0.003 | 0.052 | 0.016 |

**SHOPPING HABITS

| | CHANNEL 1 | CHANNEL 2 | CHANNEL 3 | TOTAL |
|---|---|---|---|---|
| SEGMENT 1 | 0.582 | 0.089 | 0.329 | 1.000 |
| SEGMENT 2 | 0.242 | 0.549 | 0.209 | 1.000 |
| SEGMENT 3 | 0.067 | 0.627 | 0.306 | 1.000 |
| SEGMENT 4 | 0.724 | 0.189 | 0.087 | 1.000 |
| SEGMENT 5 | 0.642 | 0.255 | 0.103 | 1.000 |

STUDY 2: CONSUMER PANEL - MARKET S
-----------------------------------

(MARKET SHARES BASED ON UNIT SALES)

| | SEGMENT 1 | SEGMENT 2 | SEGMENT 3 | SEGMENT 4 | SEGMENT 5 | TOTAL |
|---|---|---|---|---|---|---|
| SAMA | 0.264 | 0.051 | 0.005 | 0.005 | 0.012 | 0.018 |
| SALT | 0.012 | 0.015 | 0.013 | 0.017 | 0.005 | 0.014 |
| SALK | 0.079 | 0.101 | 0.004 | 0.004 | 0.011 | 0.016 |
| SARE | 0.045 | 0.023 | 0.140 | 0.105 | 0.007 | 0.097 |
| SEMI | 0.090 | 0.059 | 0.159 | 0.337 | 0.016 | 0.218 |
| SELF | 0.052 | 0.026 | 0.122 | 0.084 | 0.008 | 0.082 |
| SETA | 0.051 | 0.007 | 0.001 | 0.001 | 0.002 | 0.004 |
| SIRO | 0.030 | 0.095 | 0.003 | 0.003 | 0.644 | 0.074 |
| SIBI | 0.028 | 0.114 | 0.003 | 0.004 | 0.197 | 0.033 |
| SIRU | 0.024 | 0.013 | 0.078 | 0.062 | 0.004 | 0.056 |
| SOLD | 0.138 | 0.392 | 0.005 | 0.006 | 0.028 | 0.046 |
| SONO | 0.103 | 0.035 | 0.003 | 0.003 | 0.013 | 0.010 |
| SONY | 0.022 | 0.011 | 0.055 | 0.041 | 0.004 | 0.038 |
| SULI | 0.041 | 0.024 | 0.405 | 0.327 | 0.007 | 0.284 |
| SUSI | 0.019 | 0.034 | 0.002 | 0.002 | 0.042 | 0.009 |

| | SEGMENT 1 | SEGMENT 2 | SEGMENT 3 | SEGMENT 4 | SEGMENT 5 | TOTAL |
|---|---|---|---|---|---|---|
| INDUSTRY SALES (THOUSAND UNITS) | 76 | 200 | 705 | 1082 | 219 | 2283 |

STUDY 3: DISTRIBUTION PANEL - MARKET S
----------------------------------------

( MARKET SHARE BASED ON UNIT SALES )

|        | CHANNEL 1 | CHANNEL 2 | CHANNEL 3 | TOTAL |
|--------|-----------|-----------|-----------|-------|
| SAMA   | 0.023     | 0.010     | 0.022     | 0.018 |
| SALT   | 0.014     | 0.014     | 0.014     | 0.014 |
| SALK   | 0.015     | 0.016     | 0.018     | 0.016 |
| SARE   | 0.089     | 0.108     | 0.094     | 0.097 |
| SEMI   | 0.235     | 0.171     | 0.264     | 0.218 |
| SELF   | 0.077     | 0.090     | 0.080     | 0.082 |
| SETA   | 0.005     | 0.002     | 0.003     | 0.004 |
| SIRO   | 0.106     | 0.064     | 0.031     | 0.074 |
| SIBI   | 0.039     | 0.031     | 0.023     | 0.033 |
| SIRU   | 0.052     | 0.061     | 0.056     | 0.056 |
| SOLD   | 0.036     | 0.049     | 0.060     | 0.046 |
| SONO   | 0.012     | 0.005     | 0.014     | 0.010 |
| SONY   | 0.036     | 0.041     | 0.039     | 0.038 |
| SULI   | 0.251     | 0.329     | 0.272     | 0.284 |
| SUSI   | 0.011     | 0.008     | 0.009     | 0.009 |

| INDUSTRY SALES (THOUSAND UNITS) | 941 | 827 | 514 | 2283 |

STUDY 4: SEMANTIC SCALES - MARKET S
----------------------------------------

* THE THREE SEMANTIC DIFFERENTIAL SCALES PERCEIVED AS MOST
  IMPORTANT ARE :1. ECONOMY,2. POWER,3. DESIGN
* HIGH RATINGS CORRESPOND TO LOW ECONOMY, HIGH POWER AND
  BETTER DESIGN.

|                   | ECONOMY | POWER | DESIGN |
|-------------------|---------|-------|--------|
| IDEAL VALUE SEG.1 | 3.40    | 6.40  | 5.20   |
| IDEAL VALUE SEG.2 | 3.25    | 3.70  | 5.68   |
| IDEAL VALUE SEG.3 | 6.40    | 5.05  | 5.32   |
| IDEAL VALUE SEG.4 | 6.25    | 4.75  | 5.62   |
| IDEAL VALUE SEG.5 | 2.05    | 2.35  | 5.62   |
| SAMA              | 3.08    | 5.91  | 6.46   |
| SALT              | 6.18    | 3.25  | 6.49   |
| SALK              | 3.55    | 4.83  | 6.44   |
| SARE              | 6.32    | 5.50  | 6.46   |
| SEMI              | 5.73    | 4.68  | 6.10   |
| SELF              | 6.14    | 5.12  | 3.85   |
| SETA              | 3.67    | 6.16  | 2.73   |
| SIRO              | 2.35    | 2.07  | 6.33   |
| SIBI              | 2.84    | 2.13  | 6.25   |
| SIRU              | 6.21    | 5.21  | 6.44   |
| SOLD              | 3.15    | 4.53  | 5.50   |
| SONO              | 2.38    | 5.52  | 2.50   |
| SONY              | 6.22    | 5.43  | 6.32   |
| SULI              | 6.39    | 4.64  | 4.90   |
| SUSI              | 2.27    | 2.43  | 2.50   |

STUDY 5: PERCEPTUAL MAPPING OF BRANDS SIMILARITIES AND PREFERENCES
-----------------------------------------------------------------
                        - MARKET S -
                        --------
*STUDY REALIZED ON A RANDOM SAMPLE OF 200 INDIVIDUALS
*NO SIGNIFICANT DIFFERENCES IN PERCEPTION HAVE BEEN OBSERVED
    BETWEEN SEGMENTS
*RESULTS STATISTICALLY SIGNIFICANT HAVE BEEN OBTAINED ON TWO
    DIMENTIONS
*BASED ON SEMANTIC SCALES, THE MOST SATISFACTORY INTERPRETATION
    OF THE AXES IS :
    AXIS 1: ECONOMY (PERCEIVED ECONOMY INCREASES FROM RIGHT TO LEFT)
    AXIS 2: POWER (PERCEIVED POWER INCREASES FROM BOTTOM TO TOP)

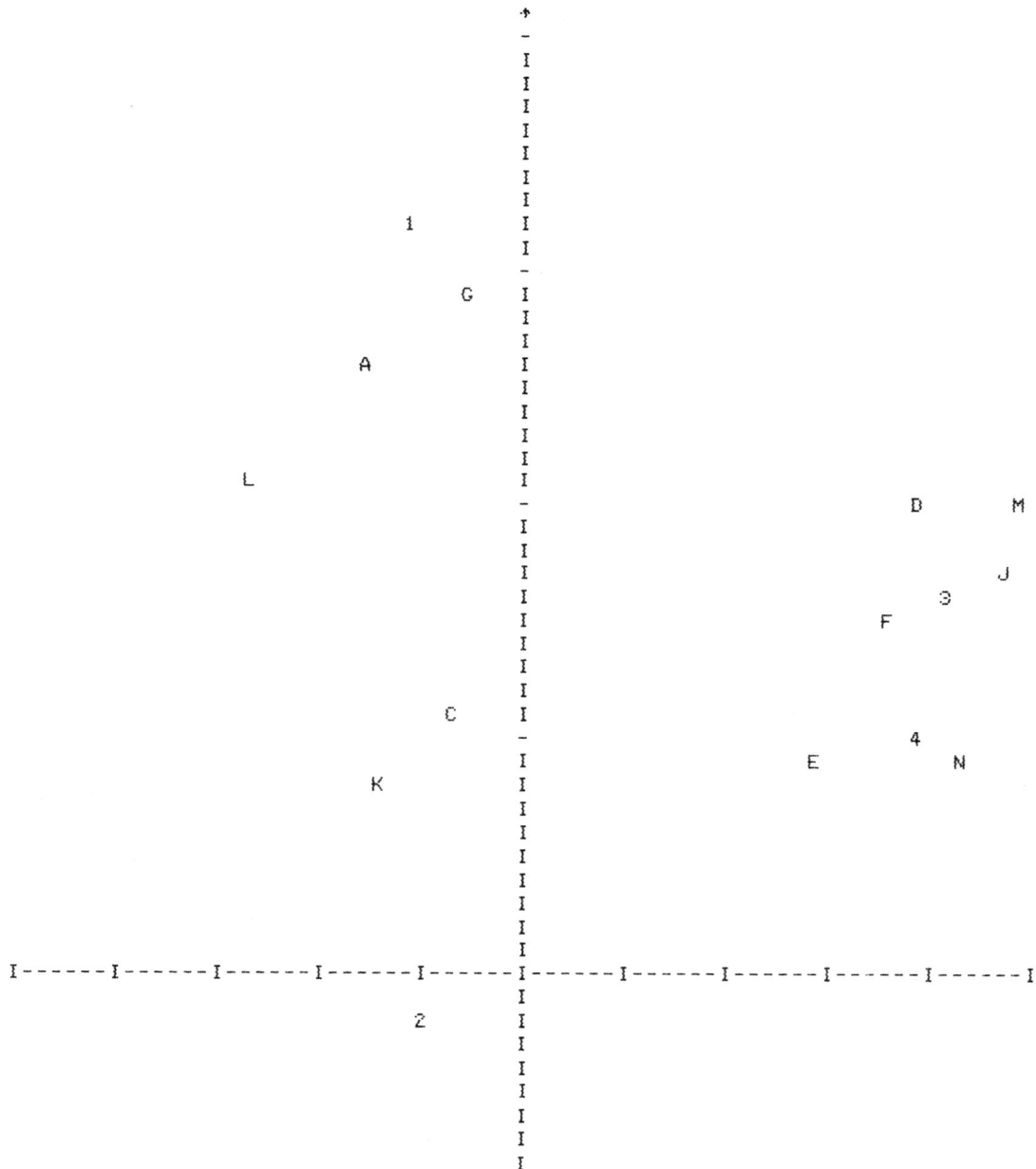

```
                                                    +
                                                    -
                                                    I
                                                    I
                                                    I
                                                    I
                                                    I
                                                    I
                                                    I
                                1                   I
                                                    I
                                                    -
                                        G           I
                                                    I
                                                    I
                                A                   I
                                                    I
                                                    I
                                                    I
                                                    I
                        L                           I                                    D       M
                                                    -
                                                    I
                                                    I
                                                    I                                        J
                                                    I                                   3
                                                    I                              F
                                                    I
                                                    I
                                                    I
                                    C               I
                                                    -                               4
                                                    I                         E           N
                            K                       I
                                                    I
                                                    I
                                                    I
                                                    I
                                                    I
                                                    I
I------I------I------I------I------I------I------I------I------I------I------I------I
                                                    I
                            2                       I
                                                    I
                                                    I
                                                    I
                                                    I
                                                    I
                                                    I
```

| IDEAL POINTS | * | SEGMENT | * | COORD.AXIS1 | * | COORD.AXIS2 | * |
|---|---|---|---|---|---|---|---|
| 1 | * | 1 | * | -4.4 | * | 15.8 | * |
| 2 | * | 2 | * | -4.2 | * | -1.0 | * |
| 3 | * | 3 | * | 16.3 | * | 7.5 | * |
| 4 | * | 4 | * | 15.5 | * | 4.8 | * |
| 5 | * | 5 | * | -13.2 | * | -11.9 | * |

| POSITIONING | * | BRAND | * | COORD.AXIS1 | * | COORD.AXIS2 | * | COMMENTS | * |
|---|---|---|---|---|---|---|---|---|---|
| A | * | SAMA | * | -6.1 | * | 12.8 | * | | |
| B | * | SALT | * | 14.5 | * | -5.0 | * | | |
| C | * | SALK | * | -3.0 | * | 5.5 | * | | |
| D | * | SARE | * | 15.5 | * | 10.0 | * | | |
| E | * | SEMI | * | 11.5 | * | 4.5 | * | | |
| F | * | SELF | * | 14.2 | * | 7.5 | * | | |
| G | * | SETA | * | -2.2 | * | 14.4 | * | | |
| H | * | SIRO | * | -11.0 | * | -12.8 | * | | |
| I | * | SIBI | * | -7.7 | * | -12.5 | * | | |
| J | * | SIRU | * | 18.6 | * | 8.1 | * | | |
| K | * | SOLD | * | -5.7 | * | 3.5 | * | | |
| L | * | SONO | * | -10.8 | * | 10.1 | * | | |
| M | * | SONY | * | 19.7 | * | 9.5 | * | | |
| N | * | SULI | * | 17.0 | * | 4.3 | * | | |
| O | * | SUSI | * | -11.5 | * | -10.5 | * | | |

```
                                      I
                                      -                          B
                                      I
                                      I
                                      I
                                      I
                                      I
                                      I
                                      I
                                      I
                                      -
                                      I
                     O                I
              5                       I
                         I            I
                  H                   I
                                      I
                                      I
                                      I
                                      I
                                      I
```

```
STUDY 6: MARKET FORECAST - MARKET S
------------------------------------
```

EXPECTED MARKET SIZE NEXT PERIOD (THOUSAND UNITS)

| SEGMENT 1 | SEGMENT 2 | SEGMENT 3 | SEGMENT 4 | SEGMENT 5 | TOTAL |
|-----------|-----------|-----------|-----------|-----------|-------|
| 72 | 210 | 916 | 1515 | 263 | 2977 |

```
STUDY 12: COMPETITIVE ADVERTISING ESTIMATES (THOUSAND $)
--------------------------------------------------------
```

| SAMA | 3635 | SALT | 2471 | SALK | 6254 | SARE | 10487 | | |
|------|------|------|------|------|------|------|-------|------|------|
| SEMI | 8133 | SELF | 8216 | VERA | 6146 | SETA | 0 | VELO | 4959 |
| SIRO | 2866 | SIBI | 2895 | SIRU | 6668 | | | | |
| SOLD | 3884 | SONO | 3855 | SONY | 4191 | | | | |
| SULI | 1940 | SUSI | 1045 | VUME | 10107 | | | | |

```
STUDY 13: COMPETITIVE SALES FORCE ESTIMATES
-------------------------------------------
```

| | CHANNEL 1 | CHANNEL 2 | CHANNEL 3 | TOTAL |
|--------|-----------|-----------|-----------|-------|
| FIRM 1 | 22 | 44 | 14 | 80 |
| FIRM 2 | 34 | 33 | 17 | 84 |
| FIRM 3 | 29 | 37 | 31 | 97 |
| FIRM 4 | 27 | 32 | 28 | 87 |
| FIRM 5 | 28 | 29 | 29 | 86 |

```
STUDY 14: SALES FORCE EXPERIMENT
--------------------------------
```
(EXPECTED RESULTS IF SALES FORCE INCREASED BY 5 IN EACH CHANNEL)

| | CHANNEL 1 | CHANNEL 2 | CHANNEL 3 |
|--------------|-----------|-----------|-----------|
| SIRO | | | |
| NUMBER DIST. | 1173 | 15379 | 1564 |
| MARKET SHARE | 0.113 | 0.068 | 0.032 |
| SIBI | | | |
| NUMBER DIST. | 1044 | 13804 | 1391 |
| MARKET SHARE | 0.042 | 0.033 | 0.025 |
| SIRU | | | |
| NUMBER DIST. | 1251 | 16463 | 1668 |
| MARKET SHARE | 0.056 | 0.064 | 0.060 |

```
STUDY 15: ADVERTISING EXPERIMENT
--------------------------------
```
(EXPECTED RESULTS IF ADV. BUDGET INCREASED BY 10% FOR GIVEN BRAND)

| | SEGMENT 1 | SEGMENT 2 | SEGMENT 3 | SEGMENT 4 | SEGMENT 5 | TOTAL |
|----------|-----------|-----------|-----------|-----------|-----------|-------|
| SIRO | | | | | | |
| AWAREN. | 0.575 | 0.555 | 0.555 | 0.553 | 0.561 | 0.574 |
| MKT.SH. | 0.030 | 0.095 | 0.003 | 0.003 | 0.647 | 0.115 |
| SIBI | | | | | | |
| AWAREN. | 0.589 | 0.579 | 0.563 | 0.567 | 0.585 | 0.587 |
| MKT.SH. | 0.028 | 0.115 | 0.004 | 0.004 | 0.201 | 0.048 |
| SIRU | | | | | | |
| AWAREN. | 0.417 | 0.409 | 0.412 | 0.408 | 0.422 | 0.406 |
| MKT.SH. | 0.027 | 0.014 | 0.088 | 0.071 | 0.005 | 0.056 |

# Appendix C
# Blank Forms

This appendix contains ten blank copies of the Decision Form, the Budgeting Form, and the Planning Form. They are to be detached and filled in as needed in the course of the simulation.

# MARKSTRAT DECISION FORM

Firm _____

Name of Commercialized Product _____

Number of R & D Projects _____     Industry _____

Number of Marketing Research Studies _____     Period _____

## PRODUCT MANAGEMENT

| Brand Names | Name of R & D Project (if modification or introduction) | Production Planning (thousand units) | Advertising Budget (thousands of $) | Advertising Research (percent) | Recommemded Retail Price ($) | Perceptual Objectives (−20 to +20, or 99) | |
|---|---|---|---|---|---|---|---|
| | | | | | | Axis 1 | Axis 2 |
| | | | | | | | |
| | | | | | | | |
| | | | | | | | |
| | | | | | | | |

## SALES FORCE

| | 1 | 2 | 3 |
|---|---|---|---|
| Distribution Channels | | | |
| Number of Salesmen | | | |

## RESEARCH AND DEVELOPMENT

| Project Name | Expenditures (thousands of $) | Physical Characteristics | | | | | |
|---|---|---|---|---|---|---|---|
| | | 1 | 2 | 3 | 4 | 5 | 6 |
| | | | | | | | |
| | | | | | | | |
| | | | | | | | |

## MARKET RESEARCH STUDIES

| | | | | | | | | | | | | | |
|---|---|---|---|---|---|---|---|---|---|---|---|---|---|

(for instructor's use)

ec(−)     ep(+)     bd(−)     bi(+)

## Modifications Resulting from Negotiations
## between the Firm and the Game Administrator

| Source of modification | Exceptional profit ($+$) or cost ($-$) (thoudands of $) | Budget increase ($+$) or decrease ($-$) (thousands of $) |
|---|---|---|
| 1. Additional information bought from the game administrator | | |
| _____ | _____ | _____ |
| _____ | _____ | _____ |
| _____ | _____ | _____ |
| 2. Inventory liquidations compensated by the game administrator | | |
| Brand: _____ | _____ | |
| Brand: _____ | _____ | |
| 3. Changes in the budget | | _____ |
| 4. Fines | _____ | _____ |
| 5. Other modifications | | |
| _____ | _____ | _____ |
| _____ | _____ | _____ |
| _____ | _____ | _____ |
| Total | | |

Signature of the firm's representative _____

Signature of the game administrator _____

# MARKSTRAT DECISION FORM

Firm _____

Name of Commercialized Product _____

Number of R & D Projects _____    Industry _____

Number of Marketing Research Studies _____    Period _____

## PRODUCT MANAGEMENT

| Brand Names | Name of R & D Project (if modification or introduction) | Production Planning (thousand units) | Advertising Budget (thousands of $) | Advertising Research (percent) | Recommemded Retail Price ($) | Perceptual Objectives (−20 to +20, or 99) | |
|---|---|---|---|---|---|---|---|
| | | | | | | Axis 1 | Axis 2 |
| | | | | | | | |
| | | | | | | | |
| | | | | | | | |
| | | | | | | | |

## SALES FORCE

| Distribution Channels | 1 | 2 | 3 |
|---|---|---|---|
| Number of Salesmen | | | |

## RESEARCH AND DEVELOPMENT

| Project Name | Expenditures (thousands of $) | Physical Characteristics | | | | | |
|---|---|---|---|---|---|---|---|
| | | 1 | 2 | 3 | 4 | 5 | 6 |
| | | | | | | | |
| | | | | | | | |
| | | | | | | | |

## MARKET RESEARCH STUDIES

| | | | | | | | | | | | | | |
|---|---|---|---|---|---|---|---|---|---|---|---|---|---|

(for instructor's use)

ec(−)     ep(+)     bd(−)     bi(+)

## Modifications Resulting from Negotiations
## between the Firm and the Game Administrator

| Source of modification | Exceptional profit (+) or cost (−) (thoudands of $) | Budget increase (+) or decrease (−) (thousands of $) |
|---|---|---|
| 1. Additional information bought from the game administrator | | |
| _____ | _____ | _____ |
| _____ | _____ | _____ |
| _____ | _____ | _____ |
| 2. Inventory liquidations compensated by the game administrator | | |
| Brand: _____ | _____ | |
| Brand: _____ | _____ | |
| 3. Changes in the budget | | _____ |
| 4. Fines | _____ | _____ |
| 5. Other modifications | | |
| _____ | _____ | _____ |
| _____ | _____ | _____ |
| _____ | _____ | _____ |
| Total | | |

Signature of the firm's representative  _____

Signature of the game administrator  _____

# MARKSTRAT DECISION FORM

Firm _____

Name of Commercialized Product _____

Number of R & D Projects _____     Industry _____

Number of Marketing Research Studies _____     Period _____

## PRODUCT MANAGEMENT

| Brand Names | Name of R & D Project (if modification or introduction) | Production Planning (thousand units) | Advertising Budget (thousands of $) | Advertising Research (percent) | Recommemded Retail Price ($) | Perceptual Objectives (−20 to +20, or 99) | |
|---|---|---|---|---|---|---|---|
| | | | | | | Axis 1 | Axis 2 |
| | | | | | | | |
| | | | | | | | |
| | | | | | | | |
| | | | | | | | |

## SALES FORCE

| Distribution Channels | 1 | 2 | 3 |
|---|---|---|---|
| Number of Salesmen | | | |

## RESEARCH AND DEVELOPMENT

| Project Name | Expenditures (thousands of $) | Physical Characteristics | | | | | |
|---|---|---|---|---|---|---|---|
| | | 1 | 2 | 3 | 4 | 5 | 6 |
| | | | | | | | |
| | | | | | | | |
| | | | | | | | |

## MARKET RESEARCH STUDIES

| | | | | | | | | | | | | | | |
|---|---|---|---|---|---|---|---|---|---|---|---|---|---|---|

(for instructor's use)

|  |
|---|

ec(−)     ep(+)     bd(−)     bi(+)

## Modifications Resulting from Negotiations
## between the Firm and the Game Administrator

| Source of modification | Exceptional profit ( + ) or cost ( − ) (thoudands of $) | Budget increase ( + ) or decrease ( − ) (thousands of $) |
|---|---|---|
| 1. Additional information bought from the game administrator | | |
| _____ | _____ | _____ |
| _____ | _____ | _____ |
| _____ | _____ | _____ |
| 2. Inventory liquidations compensated by the game administrator | | |
| Brand: _____ | _____ | |
| Brand: _____ | _____ | |
| 3. Changes in the budget | | _____ |
| 4. Fines | _____ | _____ |
| 5. Other modifications | | |
| _____ | _____ | _____ |
| _____ | _____ | _____ |
| _____ | _____ | _____ |
| Total | | |

Signature of the firm's representative _____

Signature of the game administrator _____

# MARKSTRAT DECISION FORM

Firm _____

Name of Commercialized Product _____

Number of R & D Projects _____     Industry _____

Number of Marketing Research Studies _____     Period _____

## PRODUCT MANAGEMENT

| Brand Names | Name of R & D Project (if modification or introduction) | Production Planning (thousand units) | Advertising Budget (thousands of $) | Advertising Research (percent) | Recommemded Retail Price ($) | Perceptual Objectives (−20 to +20, or 99) | |
|---|---|---|---|---|---|---|---|
| | | | | | | Axis 1 | Axis 2 |
| | | | | | | | |
| | | | | | | | |
| | | | | | | | |
| | | | | | | | |

## SALES FORCE

| | 1 | 2 | 3 |
|---|---|---|---|
| Distribution Channels | | | |
| Number of Salesmen | | | |

## RESEARCH AND DEVELOPMENT

| Project Name | Expenditures (thousands of $) | Physical Characteristics | | | | | |
|---|---|---|---|---|---|---|---|
| | | 1 | 2 | 3 | 4 | 5 | 6 |
| | | | | | | | |
| | | | | | | | |
| | | | | | | | |

## MARKET RESEARCH STUDIES

| | | | | | | | | | | | | | |
|---|---|---|---|---|---|---|---|---|---|---|---|---|---|

(for instructor's use)

ec(−)     ep(+)     bd(−)     bi(+)

## Modifications Resulting from Negotiations
## between the Firm and the Game Administrator

| Source of modification | Exceptional profit (+) or cost (−) (thoudands of $) | Budget increase (+) or decrease (−) (thousands of $) |
|---|---|---|
| 1. Additional information bought from the game administrator | | |
| | | |
| | | |
| | | |
| 2. Inventory liquidations compensated by the game administrator | | |
| Brand: | | |
| Brand: | | |
| 3. Changes in the budget | | |
| 4. Fines | | |
| 5. Other modifications | | |
| | | |
| | | |
| | | |
| Total | | |

Signature of the firm's representative  _____

Signature of the game administrator  _____

# MARKSTRAT DECISION FORM

Firm _____

Name of Commercialized Product _____

Number of R & D Projects _____     Industry _____

Number of Marketing Research Studies _____     Period _____

## PRODUCT MANAGEMENT

| Brand Names | Name of R & D Project (if modification or introduction) | Production Planning (thousand units) | Advertising Budget (thousands of $) | Advertising Research (percent) | Recommemded Retail Price ($) | Perceptual Objectives (−20 to +20, or 99) | |
|---|---|---|---|---|---|---|---|
| | | | | | | Axis 1 | Axis 2 |
| | | | | | | | |
| | | | | | | | |
| | | | | | | | |
| | | | | | | | |

## SALES FORCE

| Distribution Channels | 1 | 2 | 3 |
|---|---|---|---|
| Number of Salesmen | | | |

## RESEARCH AND DEVELOPMENT

| Project Name | Expenditures (thousands of $) | Physical Characteristics | | | | | |
|---|---|---|---|---|---|---|---|
| | | 1 | 2 | 3 | 4 | 5 | 6 |
| | | | | | | | |
| | | | | | | | |
| | | | | | | | |

## MARKET RESEARCH STUDIES

|  |  |  |  |  |  |  |  |  |  |  |  |  |
|---|---|---|---|---|---|---|---|---|---|---|---|---|

(for instructor's use)

|  |
|---|

ec(−)     ep(+)     bd(−)     bi(+)

## Modifications Resulting from Negotiations
## between the Firm and the Game Administrator

| Source of modification | Exceptional profit (+) or cost (−) (thoudands of $) | Budget increase (+) or decrease (−) (thousands of $) |
|---|---|---|
| 1. Additional information bought from the game administrator | | |
| _____ | _____ | _____ |
| _____ | _____ | _____ |
| _____ | _____ | _____ |
| 2. Inventory liquidations compensated by the game administrator | | |
| Brand: _____ | _____ | |
| Brand: _____ | _____ | |
| 3. Changes in the budget | | _____ |
| 4. Fines | _____ | _____ |
| 5. Other modifications | | |
| _____ | _____ | _____ |
| _____ | _____ | _____ |
| _____ | _____ | _____ |
| Total | | |

Signature of the firm's representative  _____

Signature of the game administrator  _____

# MARKSTRAT DECISION FORM

Firm _____

Name of Commercialized Product _____

Number of R & D Projects _____     Industry _____

Number of Marketing Research Studies _____     Period _____

## PRODUCT MANAGEMENT

| Brand Names | Name of R & D Project (if modification or introduction) | Production Planning (thousand units) | Advertising Budget (thousands of $) | Advertising Research (percent) | Recommemded Retail Price ($) | Perceptual Objectives (−20 to +20, or 99) Axis 1 | Axis 2 |
|---|---|---|---|---|---|---|---|
| | | | | | | | |
| | | | | | | | |
| | | | | | | | |
| | | | | | | | |
| | | | | | | | |

## SALES FORCE

| Distribution Channels | 1 | 2 | 3 |
|---|---|---|---|
| Number of Salesmen | | | |

## RESEARCH AND DEVELOPMENT

| Project Name | Expenditures (thousands of $) | Physical Characteristics 1 | 2 | 3 | 4 | 5 | 6 |
|---|---|---|---|---|---|---|---|
| | | | | | | | |
| | | | | | | | |
| | | | | | | | |

## MARKET RESEARCH STUDIES

| | | | | | | | | | | | | | |
|---|---|---|---|---|---|---|---|---|---|---|---|---|---|

### (for instructor's use)

| |
|---|

ec(−)     ep(+)     bd(−)     bi(+)

## Modifications Resulting from Negotiations
## between the Firm and the Game Administrator

| Source of modification | Exceptional profit ($+$) or cost ($-$) (thoudands of $) | Budget increase ($+$) or decrease ($-$) (thousands of $) |
|---|---|---|
| 1. Additional information bought from the game administrator _____ _____ _____ | _____ _____ _____ | _____ _____ _____ |
| 2. Inventory liquidations compensated by the game administrator Brand: _____ Brand: _____ | _____ _____ | |
| 3. Changes in the budget | | _____ |
| 4. Fines | _____ | _____ |
| 5. Other modifications _____ _____ _____ | _____ _____ _____ | _____ _____ _____ |
| Total | | |

Signature of the firm's representative _____

Signature of the game administrator _____

# MARKSTRAT DECISION FORM

Firm _____

Name of Commercialized Product _____

Number of R & D Projects _____     Industry _____

Number of Marketing Research Studies _____     Period _____

## PRODUCT MANAGEMENT

| Brand Names | Name of R & D Project (if modification or introduction) | Production Planning (thousand units) | Advertising Budget (thousands of $) | Advertising Research (percent) | Recommemded Retail Price ($) | Perceptual Objectives (−20 to +20, or 99) | |
|---|---|---|---|---|---|---|---|
| | | | | | | Axis 1 | Axis 2 |
| | | | | | | | |
| | | | | | | | |
| | | | | | | | |
| | | | | | | | |

## SALES FORCE

| Distribution Channels | 1 | 2 | 3 |
|---|---|---|---|
| Number of Salesmen | | | |

## RESEARCH AND DEVELOPMENT

| Project Name | Expenditures (thousands of $) | Physical Characteristics | | | | | |
|---|---|---|---|---|---|---|---|
| | | 1 | 2 | 3 | 4 | 5 | 6 |
| | | | | | | | |
| | | | | | | | |
| | | | | | | | |

## MARKET RESEARCH STUDIES

| | | | | | | | | | | | | | |
|---|---|---|---|---|---|---|---|---|---|---|---|---|---|
| | | | | | | | | | | | | | |

(for instructor's use)

ec(−)     ep(+)     bd(−)     bi(+)

## Modifications Resulting from Negotiations
## between the Firm and the Game Administrator

| Source of modification | Exceptional profit ( + ) or cost ( − ) (thoudands of $) | Budget increase ( + ) or decrease ( − ) (thousands of $) |
|---|---|---|
| 1. Additional information bought from the game administrator | | |
|     _____ | _____ | _____ |
|     _____ | _____ | _____ |
|     _____ | _____ | _____ |
| 2. Inventory liquidations compensated by the game administrator | | |
|     Brand: _____ | _____ | |
|     Brand: _____ | _____ | |
| 3. Changes in the budget | | _____ |
| 4. Fines | _____ | _____ |
| 5. Other modifications | | |
|     _____ | _____ | _____ |
|     _____ | _____ | _____ |
|     _____ | _____ | _____ |
| Total | | |

Signature of the firm's representative   _____

Signature of the game administrator   _____

# MARKSTRAT DECISION FORM

Firm _____

Name of Commercialized Product _____

Number of R & D Projects _____     Industry _____

Number of Marketing Research Studies _____     Period _____

## PRODUCT MANAGEMENT

| Brand Names | Name of R & D Project (if modification or introduction) | Production Planning (thousand units) | Advertising Budget (thousands of $) | Advertising Research (percent) | Recommemded Retail Price ($) | Perceptual Objectives (−20 to +20, or 99) | |
|---|---|---|---|---|---|---|---|
| | | | | | | Axis 1 | Axis 2 |
| | | | | | | | |
| | | | | | | | |
| | | | | | | | |
| | | | | | | | |

## SALES FORCE

|  | 1 | 2 | 3 |
|---|---|---|---|
| Distribution Channels | | | |
| Number of Salesmen | | | |

## RESEARCH AND DEVELOPMENT

| Project Name | Expenditures (thousands of $) | Physical Characteristics | | | | | |
|---|---|---|---|---|---|---|---|
| | | 1 | 2 | 3 | 4 | 5 | 6 |
| | | | | | | | |
| | | | | | | | |
| | | | | | | | |

## MARKET RESEARCH STUDIES

| | | | | | | | | | | | | | |
|--|--|--|--|--|--|--|--|--|--|--|--|--|--|

(for instructor's use)

ec(−)     ep(+)     bd(−)     bi(+)

## Modifications Resulting from Negotiations
## between the Firm and the Game Administrator

| Source of modification | Exceptional profit ( + ) or cost ( − ) (thoudands of $) | Budget increase ( + ) or decrease ( − ) (thousands of $) |
|---|---|---|
| 1. Additional information bought from the game administrator | | |
| _____ | _____ | _____ |
| _____ | _____ | _____ |
| _____ | _____ | _____ |
| 2. Inventory liquidations compensated by the game administrator | | |
| Brand: _____ | _____ | |
| Brand: _____ | _____ | |
| 3. Changes in the budget | | _____ |
| 4. Fines | _____ | _____ |
| 5. Other modifications | | |
| _____ | _____ | _____ |
| _____ | _____ | _____ |
| _____ | _____ | _____ |
| Total | | |

Signature of the firm's representative _____

Signature of the game administrator _____

# MARKSTRAT DECISION FORM

Firm _____

Name of Commercialized Product _____

Number of R & D Projects _____     Industry _____

Number of Marketing Research Studies _____     Period _____

## PRODUCT MANAGEMENT

| Brand Names | Name of R & D Project (if modification or introduction) | Production Planning (thousand units) | Advertising Budget (thousands of $) | Advertising Research (percent) | Recommemded Retail Price ($) | Perceptual Objectives (−20 to +20, or 99) | |
|---|---|---|---|---|---|---|---|
| | | | | | | Axis 1 | Axis 2 |
| | | | | | | | |
| | | | | | | | |
| | | | | | | | |
| | | | | | | | |

## SALES FORCE

| Distribution Channels | 1 | 2 | 3 |
|---|---|---|---|
| Number of Salesmen | | | |

## RESEARCH AND DEVELOPMENT

| Project Name | Expenditures (thousands of $) | Physical Characteristics | | | | | |
|---|---|---|---|---|---|---|---|
| | | 1 | 2 | 3 | 4 | 5 | 6 |
| | | | | | | | |
| | | | | | | | |
| | | | | | | | |

## MARKET RESEARCH STUDIES

|  |  |  |  |  |  |  |  |  |  |  |  |  |
|---|---|---|---|---|---|---|---|---|---|---|---|---|

(for instructor's use)

ec(−)     ep(+)     bd(−)     bi(+)

## Modifications Resulting from Negotiations
## between the Firm and the Game Administrator

| Source of modification | Exceptional profit ( + ) or cost ( − ) (thoudands of $) | Budget increase ( + ) or decrease ( − ) (thousands of $) |
|---|---|---|
| 1. Additional information bought from the game administrator | | |
| _____ | _____ | _____ |
| _____ | _____ | _____ |
| _____ | _____ | _____ |
| 2. Inventory liquidations compensated by the game administrator | | |
| Brand: _____ | _____ | |
| Brand: _____ | _____ | |
| 3. Changes in the budget | | _____ |
| 4. Fines | _____ | _____ |
| 5. Other modifications | | |
| _____ | _____ | _____ |
| _____ | _____ | _____ |
| _____ | _____ | _____ |
| Total | | |

Signature of the firm's representative  _____

Signature of the game administrator  _____

# MARKSTRAT DECISION FORM

Firm _____

Name of Commercialized Product _____

Number of R & D Projects _____     Industry _____

Number of Marketing Research Studies _____     Period _____

## PRODUCT MANAGEMENT

| Brand Names | Name of R & D Project (if modification or introduction) | Production Planning (thousand units) | Advertising Budget (thousands of $) | Advertising Research (percent) | Recommemded Retail Price ($) | Perceptual Objectives (−20 to +20, or 99) | |
|---|---|---|---|---|---|---|---|
| | | | | | | Axis 1 | Axis 2 |
| | | | | | | | |
| | | | | | | | |
| | | | | | | | |
| | | | | | | | |

## SALES FORCE

| | 1 | 2 | 3 |
|---|---|---|---|
| Distribution Channels | | | |
| Number of Salesmen | | | |

## RESEARCH AND DEVELOPMENT

| Project Name | Expenditures (thousands of $) | Physical Characteristics | | | | | |
|---|---|---|---|---|---|---|---|
| | | 1 | 2 | 3 | 4 | 5 | 6 |
| | | | | | | | |
| | | | | | | | |
| | | | | | | | |

## MARKET RESEARCH STUDIES

(for instructor's use)

ec(−)     ep(+)     bd(−)     bi(+)

## Modifications  Resulting from Negotiations
## between the Firm and the Game Administrator

| Source of modification | Exceptional profit ( + ) or cost ( − ) (thoudands of $) | Budget increase ( + ) or decrease ( − ) (thousands of $) |
|---|---|---|
| 1. Additional information bought from the game administrator | | |
| _____ | _____ | _____ |
| _____ | _____ | _____ |
| _____ | _____ | _____ |
| 2. Inventory liquidations compensated by the game administrator | | |
| Brand: _____ | _____ | |
| Brand: _____ | _____ | |
| 3. Changes in the budget | | _____ |
| 4. Fines | _____ | _____ |
| 5. Other modifications | | |
| _____ | _____ | _____ |
| _____ | _____ | _____ |
| _____ | _____ | _____ |
| Total | | |

Signature of the firm's representative  _____

Signature of the game administrator  _____

# MARKSTRAT BUDGETING FORM

Firm _____
Industry _____
Period _____

| | | | | | |
|---|---|---|---|---|---|
| Brand Name | | | | | |
| Production (units) | | | | | |
| Quantity Sold (units) | | | | | |
| Inventory (units) | | | | | |
| Retail Price ($) | | | | | |
| Average Selling Price ($) | | | | | |
| Unit Transfer Cost | | | | | |
| Revenues (thousands of $) | | | | | |
| Cost of Goods Sold (thousands of $) | | | | | |
| Inventory Costs (thousands of $) | | | | | |
| Advertising (thousands of $) | | | | | |
| Gross Marketing Contribution (thousands of $) | | | | | |

Advertising _____

R & D (thousands of $) .......... _____ R & D
Sales Force (thousands of $) .......... _____ Sales Force
Marketing Research (thousands of $) .......... _____ Marketing Research
Exceptional Cost or Profit (thousands of $) .......... 
Net Marketing Contribution (thousands of $) .......... 

Total Marketing Expenditures (thousands of $) .......... _____ Total Marketing Expenditures

# Sales Forecast Input for Budgeting

| | Total Sonite Market (thousands of units) | Total Vodite Market (thousands of units) | BRANDS Market Share (on units), Sales (thousands of units) | | | | | |
|---|---|---|---|---|---|---|---|---|
| Segment 1 | | | - - - | - - - | - - - | - - - | - - - | - - - |
| Segment 2 | | | - - - | - - - | - - - | - - - | - - - | - - - |
| Segment 3 | | | - - - | - - - | - - - | - - - | - - - | - - - |
| Segment 4 | | | - - - | - - - | - - - | - - - | - - - | - - - |
| Segment 5 | | | - - - | - - - | - - - | - - - | - - - | - - - |
| Aggregate Forecasts | | | | | | | | |

# MARKSTRAT BUDGETING FORM

Firm _____

Industry _____

Period _____

| | | | | |
|---|---|---|---|---|
| Brand Name | | | | |
| Production (units) | | | | |
| Quantity Sold (units) | | | | |
| Inventory (units) | | | | |
| Retail Price ($) | | | | |
| Average Selling Price ($) | | | | |
| Unit Transfer Cost | | | | |
| Revenues (thousands of $) | | | | |
| Cost of Goods Sold (thousands of $) | | | | |
| Inventory Costs (thousands of $) | | | | |
| Advertising (thousands of $) | | | | |
| Gross Marketing Contribution (thousands of $) | | | | |

R & D (thousands of $) ...................... _____ R & D

Sales Force (thousands of $) ...................... _____ Sales Force

Marketing Research (thousands of $) ...................... _____ Marketing Research

Exceptional Cost or Profit (thousands of $) ......................

Net Marketing Contribution (thousands of $) ......................

Total Marketing Expenditures (thousands of $) ...................... _____ Total Marketing Expenditures

Advertising _____

# Sales Forecast Input for Budgeting

| | Total Sonite Market (thousands of units) | Total Vodite Market (thousands of units) | BRANDS — Market Share (on units), Sales (thousands of units) | | | | | |
|---|---|---|---|---|---|---|---|---|
| Segment 1 | | | – – – | – – – | – – | – – – | – – | – – – |
| Segment 2 | | | – – – | – – – | – – – | – – – | – – | – – – |
| Segment 3 | | | – – | – – – | – – | – – | – – – | – – – |
| Segment 4 | | | – – – | – – – | – – – | – – – | – – – | – – – |
| Segment 5 | | | – – – | – – – | – – – | – – | – – | – – – |
| Aggregate Forecasts | | | | | | | | |

# MARKSTRAT BUDGETING FORM

Firm _____
Industry _____
Period _____

| | | | | | |
|---|---|---|---|---|---|
| Brand Name | | | | | |
| Production (units) | | | | | |
| Quantity Sold (units) | | | | | |
| Inventory (units) | | | | | |
| Retail Price ($) | | | | | |
| Average Selling Price ($) | | | | | |
| Unit Transfer Cost | | | | | |
| Revenues (thousands of $) | | | | | |
| Cost of Goods Sold (thousands of $) | | | | | |
| Inventory Costs (thousands of $) | | | | | |
| Advertising (thousands of $) | | | | | |
| Gross Marketing Contribution (thousands of $) | | | | | |

Advertising _____
R & D _____
Sales Force _____
Marketing Research _____

R & D (thousands of $) .........
Sales Force (thousands of $) .........
Marketing Research (thousands of $) .........
Exceptional Cost or Profit (thousands of $) .........
Net Marketing Contribution (thousands of $) .........

Total Marketing Expenditures _____
Total Marketing Expenditures (thousands of $) .........

# Sales Forecast Input for Budgeting

| | Total Sonite Market (thousands of units) | Total Vodite Market (thousands of units) | BRANDS Market Share (on units), Sales (thousands of units) | | | | |
|---|---|---|---|---|---|---|---|
| Segment 1 | | | - - - | - - - | - - - | - - - | - - - / - - - |
| Segment 2 | | | - - - | - - - | - - - | - - - | - - - / - - - |
| Segment 3 | | | - - - | - - - | - - - | - - - | - - - / - - - |
| Segment 4 | | | - - - | - - - | - - - | - - - | - - - / - - - |
| Segment 5 | | | - - - | - - - | - - - | - - - | - - - / - - - |
| Aggregate Forecasts | | | - - - | - - - | - - - | - - - | - - - / - - - |

# MARKSTRAT BUDGETING FORM

Firm _____
Industry _____
Period _____

| | | | | | |
|---|---|---|---|---|---|
| Brand Name | | | | | |
| Production (units) | | | | | |
| Quantity Sold (units) | | | | | |
| Inventory (units) | | | | | |
| Retail Price ($) | | | | | |
| Average Selling Price ($) | | | | | |
| Unit Transfer Cost | | | | | |
| Revenues (thousands of $) | | | | | |
| Cost of Goods Sold (thousands of $) | | | | | |
| Inventory Costs (thousands of $) | | | | | |
| Advertising (thousands of $) | | | | | |
| Gross Marketing Contribution (thousands of $) | | | | | |

Advertising ——————
R & D ——————
Sales Force ——————
Marketing Research ——————

R & D (thousands of $) ...................
Sales Force (thousands of $) ...................
Marketing Research (thousands of $) ...................
Exceptional Cost or Profit (thousands of $) ...................
Net Marketing Contribution (thousands of $) ...................

Total Marketing Expenditures ——————
Total Marketing Expenditures (thousands of $) ...................

# Sales Forecast Input for Budgeting

| | Total Sonite Market (thousands of units) | Total Vodite Market (thousands of units) | BRANDS | | | | |
|---|---|---|---|---|---|---|---|
| | | | Market Share (on units), Sales (thousands of units) | | | | |
| Segment 1 | | | - - - | - - - | - - - | - - - | - - - |
| Segment 2 | | | - - - | - - - | - - - | - - - | - - - |
| Segment 3 | | | - - - | - - - | - - - | - - - | - - - |
| Segment 4 | | | - - - | - - - | - - - | - - - | - - - |
| Segment 5 | | | - - - | - - - | - - - | - - - | - - - |
| Aggregate Forecasts | | | - - - | - - - | - - - | - - - | - - - |

# MARKSTRAT BUDGETING FORM

Firm _____
Industry _____
Period _____

| | | | | | |
|---|---|---|---|---|---|
| Brand Name | | | | | |
| Production (units) | | | | | |
| Quantity Sold (units) | | | | | |
| Inventory (units) | | | | | |
| Retail Price ($) | | | | | |
| Average Selling Price ($) | | | | | |
| Unit Transfer Cost | | | | | |
| Revenues (thousands of $) | | | | | |
| Cost of Goods Sold (thousands of $) | | | | | |
| Inventory Costs (thousands of $) | | | | | |
| Advertising (thousands of $) | | | | | |
| Gross Marketing Contribution (thousands of $) | | | | | |

Advertising _____
R & D _____
Sales Force _____
Marketing Research _____

R & D (thousands of $) ...................
Sales Force (thousands of $) ...................
Marketing Research (thousands of $) ...................
Exceptional Cost or Profit (thousands of $) ...................
Net Marketing Contribution (thousands of $) ...................

Total Marketing Expenditures

Total Marketing Expenditures (thousands of $) ...................

# Sales Forecast Input for Budgeting

| | Total Sonite Market (thousands of units) | Total Vodite Market (thousands of units) | BRANDS | | | | |
|---|---|---|---|---|---|---|---|
| | | | Market Share (on units), Sales (thousands of units) | | | | |
| Segment 1 | | | - - - | - - - | - - - | - - - | - - - |
| Segment 2 | | | - - - | - - - | - - - | - - - | - - - |
| Segment 3 | | | - - - | - - - | - - - | - - - | - - - |
| Segment 4 | | | - - - | - - - | - - - | - - - | - - - |
| Segment 5 | | | - - - | - - - | - - - | - - - | - - - |
| Aggregate Forecasts | | | - - - | - - - | - - - | - - - | - - - |

# MARKSTRAT BUDGETING FORM

Firm _____
Industry _____
Period _____

| Brand Name | | | | | |
| --- | --- | --- | --- | --- | --- |
| Production (units) | | | | | |
| Quantity Sold (units) | | | | | |
| Inventory (units) | | | | | |
| Retail Price ($) | | | | | |
| Average Selling Price ($) | | | | | |
| Unit Transfer Cost | | | | | |
| Revenues (thousands of $) | | | | | |
| Cost of Goods Sold (thousands of $) | | | | | |
| Inventory Costs (thousands of $) | | | | | |
| Advertising (thousands of $) | | | | | |
| Gross Marketing Contribution (thousands of $) | | | | | |

Advertising _____

R & D (thousands of $) ......... _____ R & D

Sales Force (thousands of $) ......... _____ Sales Force

Marketing Research (thousands of $) ......... _____ Marketing Research

Exceptional Cost or Profit (thousands of $) .........

Net Marketing Contribution (thousands of $) .........

Total Marketing Expenditures (thousands of $) ......... _____ Total Marketing Expenditures

# Sales Forecast Input for Budgeting

| | Total Sonite Market (thousands of units) | Total Vodite Market (thousands of units) | BRANDS Market Share (on units). Sales (thousands of units) | | | | | |
|---|---|---|---|---|---|---|---|---|
| Segment 1 | | | - - - | - - - | - - - | - - - | - - - | - - - |
| Segment 2 | | | - - - | - - - | - - - | - - - | - - - | - - - |
| Segment 3 | | | - - - | - - - | - - - | - - - | - - - | - - - |
| Segment 4 | | | - - - | - - - | - - - | - - - | - - - | - - - |
| Segment 5 | | | - - - | - - - | - - - | - - - | - - - | - - - |
| Aggregate Forecasts | | | - - - | - - - | - - - | - - - | - - - | - - - |

# MARKSTRAT BUDGETING FORM

Firm _____
Industry _____
Period _____

| | | | | |
|---|---|---|---|---|
| Brand Name | | | | |
| Production (units) | | | | |
| Quantity Sold (units) | | | | |
| Inventory (units) | | | | |
| Retail Price ($) | | | | |
| Average Selling Price ($) | | | | |
| Unit Transfer Cost | | | | |
| Revenues (thousands of $) | | | | |
| Cost of Goods Sold (thousands of $) | | | | |
| Inventory Costs (thousands of $) | | | | |
| Advertising (thousands of $) | | | | |
| Gross Marketing Contribution (thousands of $) | | | | |

| | |
|---|---|
| Advertising | |
| R & D | |
| Sales Force | |
| Marketing Research | |

R & D (thousands of $) ......................
Sales Force (thousands of $) ......................
Marketing Research (thousands of $) ......................
Exceptional Cost or Profit (thousands of $) ......................
Net Marketing Contribution (thousands of $) ......................
Total Marketing Expenditures (thousands of $) ......................

_____ Total Marketing Expenditures

# Sales Forecast Input for Budgeting

| | Total Sonite Market (thousands of units) | Total Vodite Market (thousands of units) | BRANDS — Market Share (on units). Sales (thousands of units) | | | | | |
|---|---|---|---|---|---|---|---|---|
| Segment 1 | | | --- \| | --- \| | - - - \| | --- \| | --- \| | --- |
| Segment 2 | | | --- \| | --- \| | --- \| | --- \| | --- \| | --- |
| Segment 3 | | | - - \| | --- \| | --- \| | --- \| | - - \| | - - |
| Segment 4 | | | --- \| | --- \| | --- \| | --- \| | --- \| | --- |
| Segment 5 | | | --- \| | --- \| | --- \| | --- \| | --- \| | --- |
| Aggregate Forecasts | | | | | | | | |

# MARKSTRAT BUDGETING FORM

Firm _____
Industry _____
Period _____

| | | | | | |
|---|---|---|---|---|---|
| Brand Name | | | | | |
| Production (units) | | | | | |
| Quantity Sold (units) | | | | | |
| Inventory (units) | | | | | |
| Retail Price ($) | | | | | |
| Average Selling Price ($) | | | | | |
| Unit Transfer Cost | | | | | |
| Revenues (thousands of $) | | | | | |
| Cost of Goods Sold (thousands of $) | | | | | |
| Inventory Costs (thousands of $) | | | | | |
| Advertising (thousands of $) | | | | | |
| Gross Marketing Contribution (thousands of $) | | | | | |

Advertising _____

R & D (thousands of $) .............. ———— R & D
Sales Force (thousands of $) .............. ———— Sales Force
Marketing Research (thousands of $) .............. ———— Marketing Research
Exceptional Cost or Profit (thousands of $) ..............
Net Marketing Contribution (thousands of $) ..............

Total Marketing Expenditures (thousands of $) .............. ———— Total Marketing Expenditures

# Sales Forecast Input for Budgeting

| | Total Sonite Market (thousands of units) | Total Vodite Market (thousands of units) | BRANDS — Market Share (on units), Sales (thousands of units) | | | | | |
|---|---|---|---|---|---|---|---|---|
| Segment 1 | | | _ _ _ / | _ _ _ / | _ _ _ / | _ _ _ / | _ _ _ / | _ _ _ / |
| Segment 2 | | | _ _ _ / | _ _ _ / | _ _ _ / | _ _ _ / | _ _ _ / | _ _ _ / |
| Segment 3 | | | _ _ _ / | _ _ _ / | _ _ _ / | _ _ _ / | _ _ _ / | _ _ _ / |
| Segment 4 | | | _ _ _ / | _ _ _ / | _ _ _ / | _ _ _ / | _ _ _ / | _ _ _ / |
| Segment 5 | | | _ _ _ / | _ _ _ / | _ _ _ / | _ _ _ / | _ _ _ / | _ _ _ / |
| Aggregate Forecasts | | | _ _ _ / | _ _ _ / | _ _ _ / | _ _ _ / | _ _ _ / | _ _ _ / |

# MARKSTRAT BUDGETING FORM

Firm _____
Industry _____
Period _____

| | | | | | |
|---|---|---|---|---|---|
| Brand Name | | | | | |
| Production (units) | | | | | |
| Quantity Sold (units) | | | | | |
| Inventory (units) | | | | | |
| Retail Price ($) | | | | | |
| Average Selling Price ($) | | | | | |
| Unit Transfer Cost | | | | | |
| Revenues (thousands of $) | | | | | |
| Cost of Goods Sold (thousands of $) | | | | | |
| Inventory Costs (thousands of $) | | | | | |
| Advertising (thousands of $) | | | | | |
| Gross Marketing Contribution (thousands of $) | | | | | |

| | Advertising |
|---|---|
| R & D (thousands of $) | R & D |
| Sales Force (thousands of $) | Sales Force |
| Marketing Research (thousands of $) | Marketing Research |
| Exceptional Cost or Profit (thousands of $) | |
| Net Marketing Contribution (thousands of $) | |
| Total Marketing Expenditures (thousands of $) | Total Marketing Expenditures |

# Sales Forecast Input for Budgeting

| | Total Sonite Market (thousands of units) | Total Vodite Market (thousands of units) | BRANDS Market Share (on units), Sales (thousands of units) | | | | | |
|---|---|---|---|---|---|---|---|---|
| Segment 1 | | | – – | – – | – – | – – | – – | – – |
| Segment 2 | | | – – | – – | – – | – – | – – | – – |
| Segment 3 | | | – – | – – | – – | – – | – – | – – |
| Segment 4 | | | – – | – – | – – | – – | – – | – – |
| Segment 5 | | | – – | – – | – – | – – | – – | – – |
| Aggregate Forecasts | | | | | | | | |

# MARKSTRAT BUDGETING FORM

Firm _____

Industry _____

Period _____

| | | | | | |
|---|---|---|---|---|---|
| Brand Name | | | | | |
| Production (units) | | | | | |
| Quantity Sold (units) | | | | | |
| Inventory (units) | | | | | |
| Retail Price ($) | | | | | |
| Average Selling Price ($) | | | | | |
| Unit Transfer Cost | | | | | |
| Revenues (thousands of $) | | | | | |
| Cost of Goods Sold (thousands of $) | | | | | |
| Inventory Costs (thousands of $) | | | | | |
| Advertising (thousands of $) | | | | | |
| Gross Marketing Contribution (thousands of $) | | | | | |

Advertising _____

R & D (thousands of $) .......... ——— R & D

Sales Force (thousands of $) .......... ——— Sales Force

Marketing Research (thousands of $) .......... ——— Marketing Research

Exceptional Cost or Profit (thousands of $) ..........

Net Marketing Contribution (thousands of $) ..........

Total Marketing Expenditures (thousands of $) .......... ——— Total Marketing Expenditures

# Sales Forecast Input for Budgeting

| | Total Sonite Market (thousands of units) | Total Vodite Market (thousands of units) | BRANDS Market Share (on units), Sales (thousands of units) | | | | | |
|---|---|---|---|---|---|---|---|---|
| Segment 1 | | | - - - \| | - - - \| | - - \| | - - - \| | - - \| | - - \| |
| Segment 2 | | | - - - \| | - - - \| | - - \| | - - \| | - - - \| | - - - \| |
| Segment 3 | | | - - \| | - - \| | - - \| | - - - \| | - - \| | - - \| |
| Segment 4 | | | - - \| | - - \| | - - \| | - - - \| | - - \| | - - \| |
| Segment 5 | | | - - \| | - - \| | - - \| | - - - \| | - - \| | - - \| |
| Aggregate Forecasts | | | | | | | | |

# MARKSTRAT PLANNING FORM

Firm _____

Industry _____

PERIODS

| | | 1 | 2 | 3 | 4 | 5 | 6 | 7 | 8 | 9 | 10 |
|---|---|---|---|---|---|---|---|---|---|---|---|
| **GENERAL PERFORMANCE** | | | | | | | | | | | |
| Turnover (millions of $) | Objective | | | | | | | | | | |
| | Outcome | | | | | | | | | | |
| Market Share (percent, on turnover) | Objective | | | | | | | | | | |
| | Outcome | | | | | | | | | | |
| Net Marketing Contribution (millions of $) | Objective | | | | | | | | | | |
| | Outcome | | | | | | | | | | |
| **MARKETING EXPENDITURES** | | | | | | | | | | | |
| Advertising (millions of $) | Objective | | | | | | | | | | |
| | Outcome | | | | | | | | | | |
| Sales Force (millions of $) | Objective | | | | | | | | | | |
| | Outcome | | | | | | | | | | |
| R & D (millions of $) | Objective | | | | | | | | | | |
| | Outcome | | | | | | | | | | |
| Marketing Research (millions of $) | Objective | | | | | | | | | | |
| | Outcome | | | | | | | | | | |
| Total Marketing Expenditures (millions of $) | Objective | | | | | | | | | | |
| | Outcome | | | | | | | | | | |
| **OTHERS** | | | | | | | | | | | |
| | Objectives | | | | | | | | | | |
| | Outcome | | | | | | | | | | |
| | Objective | | | | | | | | | | |
| | Outcome | | | | | | | | | | |

# Main Strategic Options

Indicate concisely, in terms of the elements listed below, the main strategic options on which your planning, for the remainder of the simulation is based.

Markets and Segments _____

_____

_____

Competition _____

_____

_____

Brands _____

_____

_____

Advertising _____

_____

_____

Sales Force and Distribution _____

_____

_____

Research & Developmemt _____

_____

_____

Marketing Research _____

_____

_____

Economic Environment _____

_____

_____

Others _____

_____

_____

_____

# MARKSTRAT PLANNING FORM

Firm _____

Industry _____

**PERIODS**

## GENERAL PERFORMANCE

| | | 1 | 2 | 3 | 4 | 5 | 6 | 7 | 8 | 9 | 10 |
|---|---|---|---|---|---|---|---|---|---|---|---|
| Turnover (millions of $) | Objective | | | | | | | | | | |
| | Outcome | | | | | | | | | | |
| Market Share (percent, on turnover) | Objective | | | | | | | | | | |
| | Outcome | | | | | | | | | | |
| Net Marketing Contribution (millions of $) | Objective | | | | | | | | | | |
| | Outcome | | | | | | | | | | |

## MARKETING EXPENDITURES

| | | 1 | 2 | 3 | 4 | 5 | 6 | 7 | 8 | 9 | 10 |
|---|---|---|---|---|---|---|---|---|---|---|---|
| Advertising (millions of $) | Objective | | | | | | | | | | |
| | Outcome | | | | | | | | | | |
| Sales Force (millions of $) | Objective | | | | | | | | | | |
| | Outcome | | | | | | | | | | |
| R & D (millions of $) | Objective | | | | | | | | | | |
| | Outcome | | | | | | | | | | |
| Marketing Research (millions of $) | Objective | | | | | | | | | | |
| | Outcome | | | | | | | | | | |
| Total Marketing Expenditures (millions of $) | Objective | | | | | | | | | | |
| | Outcome | | | | | | | | | | |

## OTHERS

| | | | | | |
|---|---|---|---|---|---|
| | Objectives | | | | |
| | Outcome | | | | |
| | Objective | | | | |
| | Outcome | | | | |

# Main Strategic Options

Indicate concisely, in terms of the elements listed below, the main strategic options on which your planning,
for the remainder of the simulation is based.

Markets and Segments _____

_____

_____

Competition _____

_____

_____

Brands _____

_____

_____

Advertising _____

_____

_____

Sales Force and Distribution _____

_____

_____

Research & Developmemt _____

_____

_____

Marketing Research _____

_____

_____

Economic Environment _____

_____

_____

Others _____

_____

_____

_____

_____

# MARKSTRAT PLANNING FORM

Firm _____

Industry _____

**PERIODS**

## GENERAL PERFORMANCE

| | | 1 | 2 | 3 | 4 | 5 | 6 | 7 | 8 | 9 | 10 |
|---|---|---|---|---|---|---|---|---|---|---|---|
| Turnover (millions of $) | Objective | | | | | | | | | | |
| | Outcome | | | | | | | | | | |
| Market Share (percent, on turnover) | Objective | | | | | | | | | | |
| | Outcome | | | | | | | | | | |
| Net Marketing Contribution (millions of $) | Objective | | | | | | | | | | |
| | Outcome | | | | | | | | | | |

## MARKETING EXPENDITURES

| | | 1 | 2 | 3 | 4 | 5 | 6 | 7 | 8 | 9 | 10 |
|---|---|---|---|---|---|---|---|---|---|---|---|
| Advertising (millions of $) | Objective | | | | | | | | | | |
| | Outcome | | | | | | | | | | |
| Sales Force (millions of $) | Objective | | | | | | | | | | |
| | Outcome | | | | | | | | | | |
| R & D (millions of $) | Objective | | | | | | | | | | |
| | Outcome | | | | | | | | | | |
| Marketing Research (millions of $) | Objective | | | | | | | | | | |
| | Outcome | | | | | | | | | | |
| Total Marketing Expenditures (millions of $) | Objective | | | | | | | | | | |
| | Outcome | | | | | | | | | | |

## OTHERS

| | | | | | | |
|---|---|---|---|---|---|---|
| | Objectives | | | | | |
| | Outcome | | | | | |
| | Objective | | | | | |
| | Outcome | | | | | |

## Main Strategic Options

Indicate concisely, in terms of the elements listed below, the main strategic options on which your planning,
for the remainder of the simulation is based.


Markets and Segments _____

_____

_____


Competition _____

_____

_____


Brands _____

_____

_____


Advertising _____

_____

_____


Sales Force and Distribution _____

_____

_____


Research & Developmemt _____

_____

_____


Marketing Research _____

_____

_____


Economic Environment _____

_____

_____


Others _____

_____

_____

_____

# MARKSTRAT PLANNING FORM

Firm _____

Industry _____

**PERIODS**

## GENERAL PERFORMANCE

|  |  | 1 | 2 | 3 | 4 | 5 | 6 | 7 | 8 | 9 | 10 |
|---|---|---|---|---|---|---|---|---|---|---|---|
| Turnover (millions of $) | Objective |  |  |  |  |  |  |  |  |  |  |
|  | Outcome |  |  |  |  |  |  |  |  |  |  |
| Market Share (percent, on turnover) | Objective |  |  |  |  |  |  |  |  |  |  |
|  | Outcome |  |  |  |  |  |  |  |  |  |  |
| Net Marketing Contribution (millions of $) | Objective |  |  |  |  |  |  |  |  |  |  |
|  | Outcome |  |  |  |  |  |  |  |  |  |  |

## MARKETING EXPENDITURES

|  |  | 1 | 2 | 3 | 4 | 5 | 6 | 7 | 8 | 9 | 10 |
|---|---|---|---|---|---|---|---|---|---|---|---|
| Advertising (millions of $) | Objective |  |  |  |  |  |  |  |  |  |  |
|  | Outcome |  |  |  |  |  |  |  |  |  |  |
| Sales Force (millions of $) | Objective |  |  |  |  |  |  |  |  |  |  |
|  | Outcome |  |  |  |  |  |  |  |  |  |  |
| R & D (millions of $) | Objective |  |  |  |  |  |  |  |  |  |  |
|  | Outcome |  |  |  |  |  |  |  |  |  |  |
| Marketing Research (millions of $) | Objective |  |  |  |  |  |  |  |  |  |  |
|  | Outcome |  |  |  |  |  |  |  |  |  |  |
| Total Marketing Expenditures (millions of $) | Objective |  |  |  |  |  |  |  |  |  |  |
|  | Outcome |  |  |  |  |  |  |  |  |  |  |

## OTHERS

|  |  | 1 | 2 | 3 | 4 | 5 | 6 | 7 | 8 | 9 | 10 |
|---|---|---|---|---|---|---|---|---|---|---|---|
|  | Objectives |  |  |  |  |  |  |  |  |  |  |
|  | Outcome |  |  |  |  |  |  |  |  |  |  |
|  | Objective |  |  |  |  |  |  |  |  |  |  |
|  | Outcome |  |  |  |  |  |  |  |  |  |  |

## Main Strategic Options

Indicate concisely, in terms of the elements listed below, the main strategic options on which your planning,
for the remainder of the simulation is based.

Markets and Segments _____

_____

_____

Competition _____

_____

_____

Brands _____

_____

_____

Advertising _____

_____

_____

Sales Force and Distribution _____

_____

_____

Research & Developmemt _____

_____

_____

Marketing Research _____

_____

_____

Economic Environment _____

_____

_____

Others _____

_____

_____

_____

_____

# MARKSTRAT PLANNING FORM

Firm _____

Industry _____

**PERIODS**

## GENERAL PERFORMANCE

| | | 1 | 2 | 3 | 4 | 5 | 6 | 7 | 8 | 9 | 10 |
|---|---|---|---|---|---|---|---|---|---|---|---|
| Turnover (millions of $) | Objective | | | | | | | | | | |
| | Outcome | | | | | | | | | | |
| Market Share (percent, on turnover) | Objective | | | | | | | | | | |
| | Outcome | | | | | | | | | | |
| Net Marketing Contribution (millions of $) | Objective | | | | | | | | | | |
| | Outcome | | | | | | | | | | |

## MARKETING EXPENDITURES

| | | 1 | 2 | 3 | 4 | 5 | 6 | 7 | 8 | 9 | 10 |
|---|---|---|---|---|---|---|---|---|---|---|---|
| Advertising (millions of $) | Objective | | | | | | | | | | |
| | Outcome | | | | | | | | | | |
| Sales Force (millions of $) | Objective | | | | | | | | | | |
| | Outcome | | | | | | | | | | |
| R & D (millions of $) | Objective | | | | | | | | | | |
| | Outcome | | | | | | | | | | |
| Marketing Research (millions of $) | Objective | | | | | | | | | | |
| | Outcome | | | | | | | | | | |
| Total Marketing Expenditures (millions of $) | Objective | | | | | | | | | | |
| | Outcome | | | | | | | | | | |

## OTHERS

| | | 1 | 2 | 3 | 4 |
|---|---|---|---|---|---|
| | Objectives | | | | |
| | Outcome | | | | |
| | Objective | | | | |
| | Outcome | | | | |

# Main Strategic Options

Indicate concisely, in terms of the elements listed below, the main strategic options on which your planning, for the remainder of the simulation is based.

Markets and Segments _____

_____

_____

Competition _____

_____

_____

Brands _____

_____

_____

Advertising _____

_____

_____

Sales Force and Distribution _____

_____

_____

Research & Developmemt _____

_____

_____

Marketing Research _____

_____

_____

Economic Environment _____

_____

_____

Others _____

_____

_____

_____

# MARKSTRAT PLANNING FORM

Firm _____

Industry _____

**PERIODS**

## GENERAL PERFORMANCE

| | | 1 | 2 | 3 | 4 | 5 | 6 | 7 | 8 | 9 | 10 |
|---|---|---|---|---|---|---|---|---|---|---|---|
| Turnover (millions of $) | Objective | | | | | | | | | | |
| | Outcome | | | | | | | | | | |
| Market Share (percent, on turnover) | Objective | | | | | | | | | | |
| | Outcome | | | | | | | | | | |
| Net Marketing Contribution (millions of $) | Objective | | | | | | | | | | |
| | Outcome | | | | | | | | | | |

## MARKETING EXPENDITURES

| | | 1 | 2 | 3 | 4 | 5 | 6 | 7 | 8 | 9 | 10 |
|---|---|---|---|---|---|---|---|---|---|---|---|
| Advertising (millions of $) | Objective | | | | | | | | | | |
| | Outcome | | | | | | | | | | |
| Sales Force (millions of $) | Objective | | | | | | | | | | |
| | Outcome | | | | | | | | | | |
| R & D (millions of $) | Objective | | | | | | | | | | |
| | Outcome | | | | | | | | | | |
| Marketing Research (millions of $) | Objective | | | | | | | | | | |
| | Outcome | | | | | | | | | | |
| Total Marketing Expenditures (millions of $) | Objective | | | | | | | | | | |
| | Outcome | | | | | | | | | | |

## OTHERS

| | | 1 | 2 | 3 | 4 |
|---|---|---|---|---|---|
| | Objectives | | | | |
| | Outcome | | | | |
| | Objective | | | | |
| | Outcome | | | | |

# Main Strategic Options

Indicate concisely, in terms of the elements listed below, the main strategic options on which your planning,
for the remainder of the simulation is based.

Markets and Segments _____

_____

_____

Competition _____

_____

_____

Brands _____

_____

_____

Advertising _____

_____

_____

Sales Force and Distribution _____

_____

_____

Research & Developmemt _____

_____

_____

Marketing Research _____

_____

_____

Economic Environment _____

_____

_____

Others _____

_____

_____

_____

# MARKSTRAT PLANNING FORM

Firm _____

Industry _____

**PERIODS**

## GENERAL PERFORMANCE

| | | 1 | 2 | 3 | 4 | 5 | 6 | 7 | 8 | 9 | 10 |
|---|---|---|---|---|---|---|---|---|---|---|---|
| Turnover (millions of $) | Objective | | | | | | | | | | |
| | Outcome | | | | | | | | | | |
| Market Share (percent, on turnover) | Objective | | | | | | | | | | |
| | Outcome | | | | | | | | | | |
| Net Marketing Contribution (millions of $) | Objective | | | | | | | | | | |
| | Outcome | | | | | | | | | | |

## MARKETING EXPENDITURES

| | | 1 | 2 | 3 | 4 | 5 | 6 | 7 | 8 | 9 | 10 |
|---|---|---|---|---|---|---|---|---|---|---|---|
| Advertising (millions of $) | Objective | | | | | | | | | | |
| | Outcome | | | | | | | | | | |
| Sales Force (millions of $) | Objective | | | | | | | | | | |
| | Outcome | | | | | | | | | | |
| R & D (millions of $) | Objective | | | | | | | | | | |
| | Outcome | | | | | | | | | | |
| Marketing Research (millions of $) | Objective | | | | | | | | | | |
| | Outcome | | | | | | | | | | |
| Total Marketing Expenditures (millions of $) | Objective | | | | | | | | | | |
| | Outcome | | | | | | | | | | |

## OTHERS

| | | | | | | |
|---|---|---|---|---|---|---|
| | Objectives | | | | | |
| | Outcome | | | | | |
| | Objective | | | | | |
| | Outcome | | | | | |

## Main Strategic Options

Indicate concisely, in terms of the elements listed below, the main strategic options on which your planning, for the remainder of the simulation is based.

Markets and Segments _____

_____

_____

Competition _____

_____

_____

Brands _____

_____

_____

Advertising _____

_____

_____

Sales Force and Distribution _____

_____

_____

Research & Developmemt _____

_____

_____

Marketing Research _____

_____

_____

Economic Environment _____

_____

_____

Others _____

_____

_____

_____

_____

# MARKSTRAT PLANNING FORM

Firm _____

Industry _____

**PERIODS**

## GENERAL PERFORMANCE

| | | 1 | 2 | 3 | 4 | 5 | 6 | 7 | 8 | 9 | 10 |
|---|---|---|---|---|---|---|---|---|---|---|---|
| Turnover (millions of $) | Objective | | | | | | | | | | |
| | Outcome | | | | | | | | | | |
| Market Share (percent, on turnover) | Objective | | | | | | | | | | |
| | Outcome | | | | | | | | | | |
| Net Marketing Contribution (millions of $) | Objective | | | | | | | | | | |
| | Outcome | | | | | | | | | | |

## MARKETING EXPENDITURES

| | | 1 | 2 | 3 | 4 | 5 | 6 | 7 | 8 | 9 | 10 |
|---|---|---|---|---|---|---|---|---|---|---|---|
| Advertising (millions of $) | Objective | | | | | | | | | | |
| | Outcome | | | | | | | | | | |
| Sales Force (millions of $) | Objective | | | | | | | | | | |
| | Outcome | | | | | | | | | | |
| R & D (millions of $) | Objective | | | | | | | | | | |
| | Outcome | | | | | | | | | | |
| Marketing Research (millions of $) | Objective | | | | | | | | | | |
| | Outcome | | | | | | | | | | |
| Total Marketing Expenditures (millions of $) | Objective | | | | | | | | | | |
| | Outcome | | | | | | | | | | |

## OTHERS

| | | 1 | 2 | 3 | 4 |
|---|---|---|---|---|---|
| | Objectives | | | | |
| | Outcome | | | | |
| | Objective | | | | |
| | Outcome | | | | |

## Main Strategic Options

Indicate concisely, in terms of the elements listed below, the main strategic options on which your planning. for the remainder of the simulation is based.

Markets and Segments _____

_____

_____

Competition _____

_____

_____

Brands _____

_____

_____

Advertising _____

_____

_____

Sales Force and Distribution _____

_____

_____

Research & Developmemt _____

_____

_____

Marketing Research _____

_____

_____

Economic Environment _____

_____

_____

Others _____

_____

_____

_____

# MARKSTRAT PLANNING FORM

Firm _____

Industry _____

**PERIODS**

## GENERAL PERFORMANCE

| | | 1 | 2 | 3 | 4 | 5 | 6 | 7 | 8 | 9 | 10 |
|---|---|---|---|---|---|---|---|---|---|---|---|
| Turnover (millions of $) | Objective | | | | | | | | | | |
| | Outcome | | | | | | | | | | |
| Market Share (percent, on turnover) | Objective | | | | | | | | | | |
| | Outcome | | | | | | | | | | |
| Net Marketing Contribution (millions of $) | Objective | | | | | | | | | | |
| | Outcome | | | | | | | | | | |

## MARKETING EXPENDITURES

| | | 1 | 2 | 3 | 4 | 5 | 6 | 7 | 8 | 9 | 10 |
|---|---|---|---|---|---|---|---|---|---|---|---|
| Advertising (millions of $) | Objective | | | | | | | | | | |
| | Outcome | | | | | | | | | | |
| Sales Force (millions of $) | Objective | | | | | | | | | | |
| | Outcome | | | | | | | | | | |
| R & D (millions of $) | Objective | | | | | | | | | | |
| | Outcome | | | | | | | | | | |
| Marketing Research (millions of $) | Objective | | | | | | | | | | |
| | Outcome | | | | | | | | | | |
| Total Marketing Expenditures (millions of $) | Objective | | | | | | | | | | |
| | Outcome | | | | | | | | | | |

## OTHERS

| | | 1 | 2 | 3 | 4 |
|---|---|---|---|---|---|
| | Objectives | | | | |
| | Outcome | | | | |
| | Objective | | | | |
| | Outcome | | | | |

# Main Strategic Options

Indicate concisely, in terms of the elements listed below, the main strategic options on which your planning, for the remainder of the simulation is based.

Markets and Segments _____

_____

_____

Competition _____

_____

_____

Brands _____

_____

_____

Advertising _____

_____

_____

Sales Force and Distribution _____

_____

_____

Research & Developmemt _____

_____

_____

Marketing Research _____

_____

_____

Economic Environment _____

_____

_____

Others _____

_____

_____

_____

# MARKSTRAT PLANNING FORM

Firm _____

Industry _____

**PERIODS**

## GENERAL PERFORMANCE

| | | 1 | 2 | 3 | 4 | 5 | 6 | 7 | 8 | 9 | 10 |
|---|---|---|---|---|---|---|---|---|---|---|---|
| Turnover (millions of $) | Objective | | | | | | | | | | |
| | Outcome | | | | | | | | | | |
| Market Share (percent, on turnover) | Objective | | | | | | | | | | |
| | Outcome | | | | | | | | | | |
| Net Marketing Contribution (millions of $) | Objective | | | | | | | | | | |
| | Outcome | | | | | | | | | | |

## MARKETING EXPENDITURES

| | | 1 | 2 | 3 | 4 | 5 | 6 | 7 | 8 | 9 | 10 |
|---|---|---|---|---|---|---|---|---|---|---|---|
| Advertising (millions of $) | Objective | | | | | | | | | | |
| | Outcome | | | | | | | | | | |
| Sales Force (millions of $) | Objective | | | | | | | | | | |
| | Outcome | | | | | | | | | | |
| R & D (millions of $) | Objective | | | | | | | | | | |
| | Outcome | | | | | | | | | | |
| Marketing Research (millions of $) | Objective | | | | | | | | | | |
| | Outcome | | | | | | | | | | |
| Total Marketing Expenditures (millions of $) | Objective | | | | | | | | | | |
| | Outcome | | | | | | | | | | |

## OTHERS

| | | | | | |
|---|---|---|---|---|---|
| | Objectives | | | | |
| | Outcome | | | | |
| | Objective | | | | |
| | Outcome | | | | |

# Main Strategic Options

Indicate concisely, in terms of the elements listed below, the main strategic options on which your planning. for the remainder of the simulation is based.

Markets and Segments _____
_____
_____

Competition _____
_____
_____

Brands _____
_____
_____

Advertising _____
_____
_____

Sales Force and Distribution _____
_____
_____

Research & Developmemt _____
_____
_____

Marketing Research _____
_____
_____

Economic Environment _____
_____
_____

Others _____
_____
_____
_____